The
BUDGETING
Habit

How to Make a Budget and Stick to It!

S.J. SCOTT & REBECCA LIVERMORE

ISBN-13: 978-1-946159-14-4

Disclaimer

No part of this publication may be reproduced or transmitted in any form or by any means, mechanical or electronic, including photocopying or recording, or by any information storage and retrieval system, or transmitted by email without permission in writing from the publisher.

While all attempts have been made to verify the information provided in this publication, neither the author nor the publisher assumes any responsibility for errors, omissions, or contrary interpretations of the subject matter herein.

This book is for entertainment purposes only. The views expressed are those of the author alone, and should not be taken as expert instruction or commands. The reader is responsible for his or her own actions.

Adherence to all applicable laws and regulations, including international, federal, state, and local governing professional licensing, business practices, advertising, and all other aspects of doing business in the US, Canada, or any other jurisdiction is the sole responsibility of the purchaser or reader.

Neither the author nor the publisher assumes any responsibility or liability whatsoever on the behalf of the purchaser or reader of these materials.

Any perceived slight of any individual or organization is purely unintentional.

Contents

Your Bonuses

As a way of saying thanks for your purchase, we're offering two free bonuses, which are exclusive to readers of *The Budgeting Habit*. First you will get access to a tracking spreadsheet you can use to track all your spending. And second, you will get a copy of a visual walk-through of the "You Need a Budget" software program. You can access both in the link below.

>> Go Here to Access Both Bonuses <<
www.developgoodhabits.com/budgeting-bonus

Why Me?

I walked around the lake, sobbing. In deep anguish, I yelled, "Why me, God? Why me? I don't deserve to be in this situation. I deserve better. Why did you do this to me?"

My financial situation was so dire that if it hadn't been for my kids, suicide would have been an option.

I saw no way out. In spite of the hard work of my husband and me, there just wasn't enough money to pay even the most basic bills.

I was consumed by embarrassment, fear, and guilt. The embarrassment of telling our landlord that our rent would be late. The fear of answering the phone, knowing that a creditor may be on the line.

And yes, guilt. Guilt because as much as I wanted to blame our situation on God or anyone other than ourselves, deep down I knew that our financial nightmare was our own doing.

We simply didn't manage our money well, and now the hole was so deep that there seemed to be no way out.

This is *my* story.

Perhaps you share a similar one when it comes to money.

There's a Way Out

I'm here to tell you, regardless of how deep your financial hole, it's possible to climb out. It may be dark and scary at times. You may make progress only to fall down again. But with a proper plan, there is a way out.

Thousands, if not millions—some who had dug an even deeper hole than you—have climbed out and now walk in the light of financial freedom.

I've done it. They've done it. And you can do it too!

On the other hand, maybe you're fortunate enough to *not be* in a deep financial hole. Perhaps you've seen others struggle in debt—your parents, siblings, or friends, and you know enough to want to avoid it yourself. You may be graduating from college soon or moving out on your own for the first time. Maybe the only reason you picked up this book is to learn the *right way* to handle your finances.

Or perhaps you've been on your own for a long time, and while you've done okay financially, you know there's a better way to manage your money. You may even be facing retirement, and want to make sure you can make it once your regular paycheck stops.

It doesn't matter *why* you picked up this book. What's important is that you've taken a crucial step toward building an incredibly important habit—the budgeting habit.

Living Without a Budget is Hard

Let me repeat that: Living **without** a budget is hard.

Perhaps up to this point you've thought the opposite—that living on a budget is hard.

You may have even avoided the b-word because when you hear or even think of the word, "budget," you cringe. Rebel. Resist.

Perhaps you've said or thought things like:

- "Budgets are restrictive."
- "You can't have any fun if you're on a budget."
- "I'm not about to give up my freedom!"
- "It's so hard to be on a budget!"

Let me take you back to the first words you read in this book. Do you think life was fun when my phone rang multiple times a day because I hadn't paid my bills? Was it easy when my electricity got cut off? How about when we had to tell our landlord that we didn't have all the rent money together.

Does this sound like a fun experience?

Let me tell you, it *definitely* wasn't.

Contrast that with my life now. Thanks to living on a budget, we have no debt, other than our mortgage. I quit my job and now work from home, doing something I love. We paid cash for our daughter's wedding. We spend a few months out of the year visiting my elderly mom and even work at a more relaxed pace while there. And the list goes on.

Now you tell me—is life easier with *or* without a budget?

How to Develop the Budgeting Habit

While the results of living on a budget are far easier than dealing with the results of not living on a budget, there are challenges. In fact, when we surveyed our audience prior to writing this book, people expressed the following budgeting challenges:

- Dealing with unexpected expenses (22%)
- Resisting those impulse purchases - (19%)
- Tracking their purchases - (16%)
- Being consistent with the budgeting habit - (16%)
- Managing budgets with friends and family (mostly spouses) - (13%)
- Not knowing *how* to budget - (6%)
- Generating low or irregular income - (6%)

If you've ever been hit with an unexpected expense and gone into debt because of it, succumbed to impulse buys in the checkout line, or have a spouse or friends that seem to undermine your efforts to live on a budget, you are not alone!

The good news is, none of those challenges are insurmountable, and in this book, we'll show you how to overcome any of the financial obstacles you're currently facing. No longer will you feel helpless in the area of finance. You'll get to the point where you're the master of your money, rather than allowing your money to master you.

Imagine Your Future Life

I'd like you to pause for a moment and imagine what your life will look like a year from now, five years from now, and even ten or more years after you master the budgeting habit.

What would it feel like to no longer be in debt? All the money you currently pay to credit card companies can now be spent fixing up the house, taking a vacation, or investing in your retirement fund. You celebrate the holidays without dreading the credit card bill that is sure to arrive in January.

When you walk into the furniture store, you'll know exactly how much you have to spend on that new sectional or dining set and can enjoy buying it without guilt.

You approach big and expensive life events, such as your child's college or wedding, without anxiety, knowing you've planned ahead and can pay cash.

Best of all, you approach retirement with confidence, knowing that when you finish your last day on the job, you have the time and money you need to live the life of your dreams.

Financial freedom isn't just for rich people. It's for ordinary people like me and you. And it all starts, with a simple tool known as a budget.

Welcome to "The Budgeting Habit: How to Make a Budget and Stick to It!"

In the following book, you'll discover the surprisingly simple way to master the budgeting habit. More specifically you'll learn:

- The first steps to creating a realistic budget and what to do if you have more expenses than income
- Five different budgeting approaches and how to determine which one is right for you
- How to tap into your deeper motivation and stick with your budget when you'd rather quit

- How to create small and realistic financial goals that will move you toward the bigger picture of your financial dreams
- How to turn those goals into habits so that you accomplish them without a lot of stress
- How to create an environment for success and overcome any obstacle that could derail you from sticking with your budget
- Three accountability methods to keep you on track
- How to scale up with personal challenges to speed up the process of getting out of debt, saving for a home, or investing more in your retirement fund

Budgeting is the first step to mastering your finances and in the following pages, you'll discover a step-by-step system for building this important habit.

About the Authors

This book is a collaboration between myself (Rebecca Livermore) and Steve "S.J." Scott, as part of his "Develop Good Habits" book series. While I'm narrating this book from my perspective, Steve has also incorporated many of the strategies that he's used to help tens of thousands of people build positive habits.

At the beginning of this book, I shared part of my financial story—including the painful results of not living on a budget—as well as the difference having a budget has made in my life. And like me, Steve *also* struggled with his finances before mastering this habit in his life.

In 2005, he was $15,000 in credit card debt with no job, and limited prospects for improving his financial situation. He had many sleepless nights where he thought: *How can I find a job? Where can I get extra money? How can I dig myself out of this financial hole? And how can I avoid repeating the financial mistakes that got me into this mess?*

Eventually, Steve took a similar journey to me and slowly his paid off his debt and improved his finances—mostly because he made a budget and stuck to it!

The main point of sharing our stories is to show that both Steve and I know what it's like to struggle with finances. And we also know what it's like to use the budgeting habit to get yourself out of debt and on the path to a secure financial future.

Our goal for this book is to help you master your financial future in the same way we've been able to master our own. Together we'll share many of our own experiences, as well as some stories from others who have also overcome financial challenges through the power of budgeting.

We know you're busy, so instead of filling this book with a lot of fluff, we'll get right into the nitty-gritty of how to develop the budgeting habit. Many books are filled with theory combined with golden nuggets and tell you why to make a specific change but don't tell you how to take tiny steps to grow habits for lasting results. **In the following book, we will simplify the budgeting process and provide you with a step-by-step plan to put you firmly on the path to financial freedom as quickly as possible.**

Without further ado, let's dive in!

REFLECTION QUESTIONS

Take a few minutes to think about and answer the following questions:

- Why did you buy this book?
- Have you tried budgeting before? If so, how did it go?
- What type of resistance do you feel when you think about budgeting?
- Are you willing to go all in with developing the budgeting habit?
- How does the thought of being in control of your finances make you feel?

YOUR ACTION PLAN

First, commit yourself wholeheartedly to the process of developing the budgeting habit. Let go of any financial failures from the past. Consider today to be a new day, a fresh start in your newfound commitment to squaring away your finances.

Even if you don't consider yourself to be a writer, writing things down will help you overcome many of the budgeting obstacles you'll encounter. Writing brings clarity and provides a record of your journey that you can refer to when needed.

With that in mind, jot down your answers to the reflection questions written above in a journal. The journal doesn't have to be anything fancy—even a simple composition or spiral notebook will do. Keep the journal handy because you'll use it in the coming chapters as well.

Benefits of the Budgeting Habit

When the topic of budgeting comes up, for good reason, nine times out of ten, people mention Dave Ramsey. Ramsey's appeal is that he went from wealth to bankruptcy and then back again, all with the help of a budget. According to Celebrity Net Worth, he now has a net worth of $200 million.

If you're thinking, "Well, that's Dave Ramsey, a guy who obviously knows how to make money. I never have and never will make that kind of money," consider the story of Oseola McCarty. In 6th grade, Oseola dropped out of school to care for her aunt. Following the tradition of her grandmother, she became a washerwoman, doing laundry for the wealthy. In spite of her meager income, through frugal living and careful money management, she amassed enough savings to set up a trust fund to provide college scholarships, primarily for African-American students.

Most likely you fall somewhere in between the income-producing abilities of Dave Ramsey and Oseola McCarty. Regardless of where you fall on that spectrum, how you handle the money you make is the thing that will make a difference in your quality of life and your ability to bless others financially. Budgeting is the tool to make it happen.

The Compounding Benefit of the Budgeting Habit

When you first start a budget, it may not seem to make much of a difference. In fact, you might experience frustration. You may feel like you have less money than when you weren't budgeting. But there's a simple truth that both Steve and I have experienced: Small habits lead to big results.

For example, saving $1.00 may not seem like a big deal, but with proper budgeting, even with a low income, it's possible to save $100 or more per month, $1.00 at a time.

Here are just a few things you can do with $100 per month:

- Put it into a Christmas fund, and you'll have $1,200 to spend during the holiday season without facing the dreaded credit card bill in January.

- Save $1,200 to spend on a mini-vacation. If you save $1,200 a year for a few years, you'll have enough to spend on a dream vacation.

- After one year, you'll have enough to replace a large appliance such as a refrigerator or washer and dryer.

- Build up an emergency fund to cover emergencies such as car repairs without stress.

- Put $100 per month into a retirement account. After 30 years, at a 5% annual interest rate, you'll have $80,158.81. That's obviously not enough to retire on, but it's a huge step in the right direction for such a small monthly investment.

What's the lesson here?

Well, while $100 a month might not seem like much, there's a lot you can do with this money if you commit to save a little of it every day.

Side note: To see how various investment amounts add up, check out this compound interest calculator. (Note: if you're reading this book in print, check out www.developgoodhabits.com/budgetingnotes for links to resources mentioned throughout the book.)

The Compounding Effect of Mismanaging Your Money

In the same way that there are compounding benefits to using a budget to manage your money well, the negative impact of not budgeting also compounds over time. To illustrate this point, think about how most people pay for things—putting it on a credit card. Let's say you have a credit card balance of $5,000 with an interest rate of 15%, if you pay $100 per month, it will take 79 months to pay it off. And that's assuming you don't charge anything else! **That $5,000 of stuff ends up costing $7,900.**

See how the compounding effect can derail your budgeting efforts?

Side note: If you want to know how long it'll take to pay off your existing credit card balances, then I recommend checking out the credit card payoff calculator provided by the Bank Rate website.

Now, if you ignore the negative compounding effect, you might have to deal with a number of challenging issues like:

1) Having no money to buy your children holiday and birthday presents. Either you disappoint your kids, or you run up the credit card—and spend the rest of the year paying it off.

2) Not being able to take a vacation—ever.

Or you could experience embarrassment through things such as:

- Creditors calling
- Driving a crappy car that's always breaking down
- Inadequate back-to-school clothing for your kids
- Not having money to do things with your friends
- Insecurity, particularly when facing job loss or retirement
- Getting deeper into credit card debt

While having a substantial income helps, the next time you think that you'll never pay off your debt with your current salary, remember the story of Oseola McCarty. Despite her meager income, through careful budgeting, she met her own financial needs *and* blessed others financially.

REFLECTION QUESTIONS

- If you had to pick just one thing to do with an extra $1,200 a year, what would you choose?

- What was a specific incident in your past where financial mismanagement caused you embarrassment?

- Were you surprised to learn that Oseola McCarty was able to establish a scholarship fund in spite of her humble income level? How does her story make you think differently about your potential to bless others financially?

- How has a lack of budgeting impacted those you love, such as your children?

- Have you ever calculated the true cost of your credit card debt?

YOUR ACTION PLAN

First, create a vision board or write in your journal to illustrate how budgeting will change your life and the lives of those you love. Don't be afraid to dream big!

Is there a travel destination you've always wanted to go to? What about gifts you'd like to give your children? Do you dream of buying a home or renovating your current home? How about putting your children through college, debt free? Do you dream of retiring early? Perhaps like Oseola McCarthy, you dream of helping those less fortunate.

Regardless of your dreams, create a visual or written declaration that illustrates your financially abundant dream life.

Next, get out a piece of paper and write about an embarrassing financial incident from your past. It could be anything from bounced checks to creditors calling, or your children being embarrassed by having to wear old, worn out clothing or shoes on the first day of school. Be sure to include how you felt during the incident. Then, crumple up the paper and throw it out as a symbolic gesture that those days are over, and you refuse to live that way from here on out.

Now it's time to write your future reality as if it's already happened. For instance, write about taking your kids shopping for new school clothing, and how confident you felt when you paid for them without going into debt. Describe their excitement as they got dressed on the first day of school and how proud they were when you dropped them off. Since this is something you're looking toward, instead of writing it on a loose piece of paper, write it in something more permanent such as your journal or Evernote.

After that, make amends to anyone you've hurt as a result of mismanaging your finances. Apologize and ask for forgiveness. If you find it hard to do face-to-face, or if you don't have a way to connect in person, write a letter.

Finally, select an item you'd like to purchase in the future, such as a new appliance or piece of furniture. Using the credit card calculator, compare the cost of paying cash to taking one, three or five years to pay off the item.

Getting Started with the Budgeting Habit

Have you tried budgeting before only to give up a few days later? Don't worry if you said "yes" to this question. The good news is the framework we provide in this book will help you create a simple budget and stick to it. But to get started, we recommend completing a few key action steps...

Your First Steps

To begin, you need to calculate the real numbers on your current income, debt, and expenses.

This is often a sobering and, in some cases, downright scary thing to face. In fact, both Steve and I remember how much anxiety this step caused us when we finally decided to face the facts about our finances. So, put on some comfy clothes, and soft relaxing music and grab a bottle of wine or beverage of choice before you get started.

If you're single, you can do this alone, but if you're in a relationship with shared finances, be sure to include your partner. Commit ahead of time to not criticize or point fingers at your partner for any less-than-ideal aspects of your financial state.

Gather a Few Supplies

You need just a small number of items to get started:

- Your comfort items (e.g., that bottle of wine mentioned earlier!).
- We've provided a free spending-tracking spreadsheet which you can get here. Or if you prefer, you can use pencil and paper.
- A list of your income from the past 12 months. This could be in the form of check stubs or deposits to your bank account(s).
- Bank and credit card statements for all accounts.

Calculate Your Income

Write down all your income sources. Be sure to include everything, such as income from your spouse and any contributing family members.

Next, calculate your total monthly income. If your income is the same every month, this step is easy. Simply add up the total amount of your household income for the month. If your income varies each month, calculate your average monthly household income by adding up your monthly income for the past 12 months and dividing by 12.

Calculate Your Expenses by Category

This is the most time-consuming part of the process. It can also be the most sobering. As painful as this may be, don't skip this step or fudge on the numbers. It's not time to beat yourself up, but it is time to face the reality of where your money has gone over the past several months. This step empowers you to know how much to allocate to your various budget categories, and when needed, where to cut back.

Write Down Every Expenditure

Go through your credit card and bank account statements and write down all of your expenditures for, at a minimum, the past three to six months.

For example, if by looking at your bank statement you see that last month you spent $196.72 on groceries week one, $127.35 on week two, $167.86 on week three, and $194.78 on week four, your total cost of groceries last month was $686.71. You may also find that last month you spent a total of $487.32 on eating out, $47.35 going to the movies, $128.36 on your electric bill and so on.

Ideally, go back an entire year. Looking back over the past year gives you a more complete picture because it includes things that happen once or a few times a year such as holidays, birthdays, and home and car maintenance.

This is a big task and may seem overwhelming. Take it one month at a time, and plan to take a break and get up and move around a bit after completing a few months' worth of entries.

Remember to use the complimentary spreadsheet we provided: www.developgoodhabits.com/budgeting-bonus

(Note that we modeled our categories after the ones in *You Need a Budget* as that's the program we recommend, but feel free to adapt the categories to your specific needs.)

Create an "Elephant Habit" to Write Down Your Expenses

If you feel overwhelmed by the idea of dedicating an entire day to writing down your expenses, then you can use the "elephant habit" strategy that Steve covers in his book, *Habit Stacking*.

Let me explain:

Whenever you're faced with a large, complex goal, all you need to do is chip away at it in small chunks. Like the adage about eating an elephant one bite at a time.

Unfortunately, many people don't apply this mindset to their lives. When they're forced to tackle large projects, they procrastinate or even avoid them completely because the tasks seem insurmountable.

Elephant habits are designed to overcome the natural resistance that we all feel whenever we're forced to do a potentially unpleasant task. You know it must be done, but you avoid starting because dedicating a few days to it sounds as fun as getting a root canal.

The purpose of an elephant habit is to chip away at a simple but time-consuming project in five- to ten-minute daily increments. This is perfect for writing down your expenditures because you can break the process down into a daily task where you do the calculations for one month. So in twelve days, you'll have calculated all of your expenses for the past year.

Now, when calculating your monthly expenses, you should break them down into five primary categories.

#1. Monthly Priorities

These are the expenditures that you feel are personal necessities. There is no right answer for what's a priority – just make sure that these are expenditures that you absolutely *have to* pay for each month. Here are a few items that you might consider for this category:

- Rent/Mortgage
- Electric
- Water
- Trash
- Internet
- Groceries
- Transportation
- Interest and Fees
- Netflix/Hulu/Amazon Prime

#2. True Expenses

True expenses are those that occur less frequently but that you ideally save up for over time so that you have the money available when needed. Sinking funds is another name for true expenses. For example:

- Auto Maintenance
- Home Maintenance
- Renter's/Home Insurance
- Medical
- Clothing
- Gifts (holidays, birthdays, anniversary, weddings, etc.)

- Giving
- Computer Replacement
- Software Subscriptions
- Savings and Investments

#3. Debt Payments

Unfortunately, we live in a debt-based economy. So, if you're like most people, then a sizeable portion of your budget will be dedicated to debt payments like:

- Student Loans
- Auto Loans
- Credit Card Payments

#4. Quality of Life Investments

One of the best investments you can make is in yourself. That's why we feel you should do your best to spend money in a few areas like:

- Vacation
- Fitness
- Education
- Health and wellness

#5. Fun Experiences

Finally, you should consider setting aside money for enjoyable experiences that help relieve some of the daily pressures that you regularly experience, like:

- Dining Out
- Babysitting (If you and your partner need "quality time" away from the little ones.)
- Gaming
- Music
- Movies
- Fun Money

Add Up Your Expenditures

Now it's time to add up your expenditures and calculate what you spend, on average, each month. If you used the spreadsheet we provided you, take a look at column O to see how much you spend on average in each category. You'll find your average total monthly expenditure amount at the bottom of the spreadsheet.

Manual Calculation

If you opted to use pencil and paper instead of the spreadsheet, here's how to manually calculate your average monthly expenditures.

First, add up what you spent each month in each of the following categories:

1) Monthly Priorities
2) True Expenses

3) Debt Payments

4) Quality of Life Investments

5) Fun Experiences

Next, add up your total expenditures for each month. For example, if in January you spent $1,900 on monthly priorities, $700 on true expenses, $400 on debt payments, $450 on quality of life, and $400 on just for fun, your total expenditures for January add up to $3,850.

Third, calculate your average monthly expenditures. Add up your total expenditures for each of the 12 months and then divide this number by 12 to find out how much you spend in an average month.

Finally, it's time to compare your average monthly income with your average monthly expenditures. If you've been relying on your credit card to cover some of your expenses, you may find that you spent more than you made over the past year.

If that's the case, don't panic! The following steps will help you create a realistic budget that has you spending less than you make each month.

Needs vs. Wants

The first step in getting your budget under control is differentiating between needs and wants. For instance, paying your electric bill each month is a need, but going out to lunch every day with your coworkers is likely a want.

If you're using the spreadsheet, in sheet two, input the figures for only the essential items. This is your bare-bones budget. Compare the total monthly figure for your bare-bones budget with your average monthly income. Little by little add in extra items to the quality of life and just for fun categories, until your income and outgo numbers match.

The Goldilocks Guide to Budgeting

Chances are you've heard the story of Goldilocks. In the story, one bed was too hard, one was too soft, and one was just right. A bare-bones budget that has no room for anything other than essentials is too hard. That's a painful "bed" to stay in very long. If you spend more than you make, that bed is too soft. The goal, then, is a bed (or a budget) that is just right. A just right budget has enough cushion to make life comfortable and fun but isn't so soft that it's hard to get out of.

Bare Bones Budget

By the way, if you find that your bare-bones budget takes up most of your income, you need to get out of that uncomfortable place as soon as possible. You may need to temporarily take on an extra job to pay off debt, sell a car, or move to a less-expensive home or apartment to speed things up.

If you have a family, be sure to involve them in decisions regarding budget cuts. Ask each family member what one thing matters most and do whatever you can to keep those things in the budget, at a reduced or modified level if needed.

For example, if a weekly movie and dinner out is a high priority for your spouse, ask which matters most—the dinner or the movie. If both matter equally, suggest cutting back to a monthly, rather than weekly dinner and movie night. Better yet, if your spouse typically does the cooking, offer to cook once a week. While you're cooking, your spouse can scour Amazon or Netflix for a movie to watch after dinner.

Sacrifices Don't Have to Last Forever

Perhaps you're facing some painful sacrifices. If so, you're not alone. Many people have gone before you.

In fact, at one of my lowest points, my husband and myself with our two kids and family dog, moved from a large home in an exclusive neighborhood into a small low-income apartment. I still remember the pain of that decision, and the tears shed as I got rid of most of our belongings in preparation for the move.

That drastic measure laid the foundation for a new level of financial freedom we still enjoy today. Within a month after moving, both I and my husband got new jobs. We stayed in the apartment for three years while we paid off debt and saved up for a home of our own.

REFLECTION QUESTIONS

- How did you feel after adding up your income and expenses? Did you feel encouraged or hopeless? If you feel discouraged, know that budgeting is a way of telling yourself the truth about your financial situation, and knowing the truth is the first step in working toward financial freedom.

- Which of the items you typically spend money on are actual needs vs. wants?

- If you have more expenses than income, what sacrifices are you willing to make to balance things out?

YOUR ACTION PLAN

Schedule a time to calculate your income and expenses as detailed earlier in this chapter. Here's a brief recap of the process:

- Gather supplies such as the spreadsheet or paper and pen, as well as documentation of your income and expenses such as bank statements.
- Add up all of your income.
- Add up all of your expenses by category (groceries, house payment or rent, utilities, etc.).
- Compare your income with your expenses.

If your expenses are greater than your income, or if you want to free up more money to save or invest, differentiate between your needs and wants and eliminate or reduce unnecessary items until the figures line up the way you want. Remember that sacrifices don't necessarily have to last forever.

If you need to bring in extra income at least temporarily, brainstorm a list of at least five ways to make some fast cash.

If you're married or share finances with a significant other, be sure to involve them in the process. Make a commitment ahead of time to listen carefully and consider their feelings.

After you've gone through this process, you may feel a little beat up or discouraged. Remind yourself that these unpleasant feelings are normal when you face the truth of your financial situation, but they will ultimately lead to freedom.

Finally, break out your journal once again and write about your financial future where your income exceeds your expenses as if it's already a reality. Give yourself permission to dream big, knowing full well that as you begin to handle your money wisely, your financial situation will improve.

5 Popular Budgeting Strategies

After calculating your income and expenses, you should select a specific budgeting model to follow. There are dozens, even hundreds of budgeting approaches – each with their own pros and cons. But for the sake of simplicity, we recommend picking one of the following five popular strategies.

Strategy #1: The 50/30/20 Approach

Initially proposed by Harvard economist (and current U.S. senator) Elizabeth Warren and her daughter, Amelia Warren Tyagi, the 50/30/20 budgeting approach allocates net income by the following percentages:

- 50% on necessities (e.g., house payment or rent, food, utilities, gas, car payment)
- 30% on wants (dinner out, movies, etc.)
- 20% into savings/investing/paying off debt

The biggest benefit of this approach is that it provides a balanced approach to ensure that you cover needs, wants, future expenses and goals.

The biggest con is that the percentages don't work for everyone, particularly lower income people who may need to spend more than 50% of their net income on essentials.

Strategy #2: The 80/20 Budgeting Method

Like the 50/30/20 approach, the 80/20 budgeting approach allocates net income by percentages, but it's a much less-detailed approach. With this approach, as soon as you get paid, put 20% of your net income into savings and spend the remaining 80% as desired.

The benefit of this approach is that it takes very little time to implement and doesn't require any tracking.

The biggest drawback about this strategy is it doesn't take into account large, periodic expenditures such as quarterly car insurance payments, Christmas, back-to-school clothing, and so on. When those big expenses come up, you may not have enough to cover them without dipping into your savings account.

This approach is only advisable for those who are not at all detail oriented and simply won't keep up with tracking. If you choose this approach, be sure to pay for your essential expenses such as rent, utilities, and groceries immediately after payday. You may also wish to increase your savings percentage from 20—25%, so you have money on hand to pay for infrequent or unexpected expenses.

> **Side note:** The 80/20 budgeting method is purely based on allocating income by those percentages and is not to be confused with the 80/20 rule that is also referred to as the Pareto Principle, which Steve frequently covers in his books.

Strategy #3: Envelope System

With the envelope system, instead of using a credit or debit card, you use cash. After creating your budget based on something like the 50/30/20 approach, divide your cash into envelopes based on category. For instance, put cash for groceries into the grocery envelope. When you go to the grocery store, pull cash out of that envelope to pay for groceries.

The envelope system works best for categories where you may be tempted to blow your budget, such as groceries, eating out, and entertainment. The genius of this approach is that when the money's gone, you stop spending. It also makes you more mindful of your spending.

For instance, if you're in the grocery store and you only have $100 in your grocery envelope, you count the cost of each item you put in your cart to make sure that the total doesn't exceed the amount in the envelope.

With the envelope system, the level of tracking you do is up to you. At the most basic level, the only tracking needed is to occasionally count the money in the envelope and see how much you have left to spend. One step up is to put all receipts into the appropriate envelope. Others use the outside of the envelope as a register where they record the money they put into the envelope, as well as all expenditures.

Many find they spend more wisely and cautiously when using cash than they do when paying for everything with a debit or credit card. Using cash curbs impulse buys—particularly if you have to go home to get your cash before making a purchase.

But there are some drawbacks to this approach. First off, if your envelopes are lost or stolen, the money is gone. Because of that, you may not want to carry all that cash with you all the time. You then have to remember to take cash with you every time you go to shops, restaurants, the movie theater, etc.

The envelope system may also be more challenging for couples, since only one person may have the cash on hand. Possible workarounds for couples are splitting the cash between each spouse or making each spouse responsible for different spending categories. Envelopes can also be bulky, which is challenging for men, or women who don't carry large purses. My husband solved this problem by dividing cash in his wallet with different colored paper clips.

While there are drawbacks to this approach, it's ideal for those who struggle with overspending, are trying to get out of debt, or are prone to bouncing checks.

Strategy #4: Zero-Based Budgeting

Zero-based means that your income minus expenses equals zero. This doesn't mean that you end up with $0.00 in your checking account, but that you account for every penny of income and expenses.

The most significant benefit of zero-based budgeting is that you give every dollar a job. This makes you more mindful of your spending.

The biggest con is that since zero-based budgeting is more detailed, it takes more time than some of the other budgeting approaches.

Strategy #5: Automation

Many find it helpful to automate certain aspects of the budgeting process. For instance, you may automatically move a certain dollar amount from checking into savings each month or sign up for an employer-sponsored investment plan. The key here is to use technology to remove most of the guesswork and decision-making on your part— each month, money comes out of your account and goes into specific "budget buckets."

The biggest advantage of this strategy is you don't have to make money decisions, besides reviewing these withdrawals each month to make sure you're allotting the correct amount of money.

On the other hand, a major disadvantage is you might become financially lazy. When everything is done for you, you'll stop monitoring all your accounts and not know exactly where your money is going.

Mix and Match

The great thing about these different budgeting approaches is that you can mix and match them.

For instance, you can use zero-based budgeting with the 50/30/20 budget where you create three broad categories for your finances, but also track every dollar to ensure you know where your money is being spent.

Or you can combine the 50/30/20 budget with the envelope system, by using cash to pay for items that fit into the 30% (wants) category.

Overall though, *all* these budgeting systems will work—either individually or when combined. The trick to making them work *for you* is to make a plan and commit to sticking with it!

REFLECTION QUESTIONS

- What was your gut reaction as you read about the different budgeting approaches? Did some resonate with you, while others made you shake your head and say, "No way!"?

- Are you a detailed person or do you prefer to fly by the seat of your pants?

- Do you struggle with tracking expenses such as entering information into a spreadsheet or app?

- Do you have a tendency to bounce checks?

- Are you commonly tempted by impulse buys?

YOUR ACTION PLAN

In your journal, write out the answers to the questions listed above.

One thing: The only wrong answers are dishonest ones, so don't claim (even to yourself) that you're detailed oriented, when the reality is that you hate keeping track of things.

It's important to be extremely honest here because this will help you clearly identify the type of budgeting system that works best for you.

In light of that, choose one or two options you think you can implement.

For instance, if you're detailed oriented, you may want to combine the zero-based budget approach with the 50/30/20 approach.

On the other hand, if you prefer to fly by the seat of your pants, then the 80/20 budget combined with automation may be your best bet.

Or if you have a tendency to bounce checks, then using the cash envelope system for everything other than your main bills may be the best option.

The key step here is to pick a method or combination of methods that suits your personality and needs.

Describe in writing your ideal budget approach. Include whether or not you plan to combine any of the approaches such as the 50/30/20 approach with the envelope system.

Now let's dive in to the eight steps to developing the budgeting habit.

Step 1: Connect Budgeting to Your Purpose

If you try to build the budgeting habit just because you think you should, you'll likely fail.

To increase your odds of budgeting success, you want to attach this habit to a goal that's personally important to you. Connecting to your purpose matters because challenges will come, and it's difficult to stick with something challenging like budgeting for the long haul if you don't have a deeper purpose.

Discover Your Underlying Reason

The first step in this process is to connect with the underlying reason of why you'd like to build the budgeting habit.

For example, you may want to build the budgeting habit to eliminate all of your personal debt. The question you must ask yourself is why does that matter? What's your purpose in eliminating debt?

Here are a few examples:

- Reduce stress in your life because you won't worry as much about bills every month

- Move into a new career because you won't "need" that current job as much to pay the bills

- Break bad habits related to a specific aspect of your spending

- Save up for a dream vacation
- Save money to put into a long-term investment
- Start a "side hustle" that can replace your job
- Become financially free to support your family through passive income

Consider Your Biggest Financial Pain Points

One of the best ways to connect with your why for building the budgeting habit is to recognize the pain not having this habit brings. Consider both your past experiences, as well as the future pain you'll experience if you don't budget.

Here are some example questions to ask yourself:

- What's your current biggest frustration with budgeting (or the results of not having a budget)?
- How have you—and people you love—been impacted by a lack of a budget?
- What are your biggest financial regrets?
- Do you feel financially unprepared for significant life events such as weddings (your own or your children's), buying a home, and retirement?
- How can budgeting reduce or eliminate the painful consequences of irresponsible spending?
- What bad habits related to spending do you want to break?

Again: There isn't a wrong answer to any of these questions. The goal of this exercise is to identify the specific mental blocks that *you* currently experience when it comes to spending money.

Your Version of Financial Freedom

Financial freedom looks different for everyone. Some define financial freedom as retiring young. Others want to work until the traditional retirement age, and then have enough saved to pay for living expenses and enjoy hobbies without stress. Others might want to buy a big house in the "right" neighborhood, while some prefer to live in a tiny house and work part-time.

None of these motivations are right or wrong, so as you consider your deeper purpose, let go of what you think you *should* do, and embrace what truly matters most to you.

REFLECTION QUESTIONS

- What's the #1 reason you want to develop the budgeting habit? Is it because you're tired of the stress, fear, and embarrassment that not having a budget has caused? Is it because you are approaching retirement and don't have enough saved? Or is it something even deeper such as changing your family history, so that your children and future grandchildren will benefit from your example?

- How would you describe financial freedom?

- How has not budgeting impacted you in the past?

- What impact will budgeting have on your present and future?

- How far are you willing to go to make your financial dreams a reality?

YOUR ACTION PLAN

Remember, if you try to build the budgeting habit just because you think you should, you'll likely fail, so take the time to dig deeper into why budgeting matters to you and how it will impact not just you, but other members of your family.

It's time to break out your journal again and write about at least two of the reflection questions listed above. If you choose to write about the positive impact of budgeting, such as financial freedom and the impact that budgeting will have on your financial future, remember to write it as if it's already a reality. Doing so will help you feel the positive impact of the decision and help you change the way you think about money in general, particularly budgeting.

Step 2: Create a Money-Specific S.M.A.R.T. Goal

There's a difference between goals and habits. A goal is a broad outcome that you want to achieve in your life. Your goal enables you to connect with your purpose and is the transformation you want to experience. A habit is a day-to-day execution on the goal. Habits aren't as sexy as goals, but your daily habits ultimately determine what you achieve in life.

Make Your Money Goal S.M.A.R.T.

When it comes to goal setting, our suggestion is to set S.M.A.R.T. goals for every quarter (i.e., three months) instead of the year-long goals that most people create.

To begin, let's start with a simple definition of S.M.A.R.T. goals.

George Doran first used the S.M.A.R.T. acronym in the November 1981 issue of the *Management Review*. It stands for:

- Specific;
- Measurable;
- Attainable;
- Relevant; and
- Time-bound.

Specific

Specific goals answer your six "W" questions:

- Who?
- What?
- When?
- Where?
- Which?
- Why?

When you can identify each element, you'll know which tools (and actions) are required to reach a goal:

- Who is involved?
- What do you want to accomplish?
- When do you want to do it?
- Where will you complete the goal?
- Which requirements and constraints might get in your way?
- Why are you doing it?

Specificity is necessary because when you reach these milestones (date, location, and objective), you'll know for sure you have achieved your goal.

Measurable

Measurable goals are defined with precise times, amounts, or other units—essentially anything that measures progress toward a goal.

Creating measurable goals makes it easy to determine if you have progressed from point A to point B. Measurable goals also help you figure out when you're headed in the right direction and when you're not. Generally, a measurable goal statement answers questions starting with *how*, such as:

- How much?
- How many?
- How fast?

Attainable

Attainable goals stretch the limits of what you think is possible. While they're not impossible to complete, they're often challenging and full of obstacles. The key to creating an attainable goal is to look at your current life and set an objective that seems *slightly* beyond your reach. That way, even if you fail, you still accomplish something of significance.

Relevant

Relevant goals focus on what you truly desire. They are the exact opposite of inconsistent or scattered goals. They are in harmony with everything that is important in your life, from success in your career to happiness with the people you love.

Time-Bound

Time-bound goals have specific deadlines. You are expected to achieve your desired outcome before a target date. Time-bound goals are challenging and grounding. You can set your target date for today, or you can set it for a few months, a few weeks, or a few years from now. The key to creating a time-bound goal is to set a deadline you'll meet by working backward and developing habits (more on this later).

Side note: Okay, here's where it might get confusing. Sometimes the "three-month rule" doesn't apply to every situation. Occasionally, you'll have a major goal that demands your attention but doesn't neatly fit into a quarterly block of time.

For instance, you may have a goal of paying off a huge amount of credit card debt, or your mortgage, goals that are too big to accomplish in three months. Despite the fact that you can't accomplish the goal in three months, working toward the goal is still a critical part of each day.

The point here is like everything else in this book, the three-month rule isn't written in stone. Use it as a general guideline—not as an absolute must.

Nine Examples of S.M.A.R.T. Money Goals

To briefly demonstrate this concept, here are nine S.M.A.R.T. goals related to money and the budgeting habit:

1) **Tracking:** I will spend a minimum of five minutes each day reviewing my budget and entering any transactions for the day. I'll do this immediately after dinner.

2) **Debt Payoff:** I will pay off my Chase Visa card by June 15th.

3) **Debt Payoff:** I will pay off *all* credit card debt by the end of this year.

4) **Savings:** I will put $1,000 in an emergency fund by April 30th.

5) **Savings:** I'll grow my emergency fund to $5,000 by June 1st next year.

6) **Savings:** I will save up $1,200 to spend on Christmas gifts by November 1st.

7) **Savings:** I will save up $20,000 for a down payment on a home in the next five years. (Give a specific date.) To stay on track with this goal, I'll save a minimum of $300 each month.

8) **Investing:** I will save 10% of every paycheck and invest it in index funds through Vanguard.

9) **Investing:** I will max out my Roth IRA by December 31st by investing $250 out of each paycheck.

See how I listed specific goals? That's what you need to set S.M.A.R.T. goals! The purpose here is to create something where you'll know, without a doubt, when you have achieved a certain outcome. There is no ambiguity—either you have or haven't reached each of your goals.

REFLECTION QUESTIONS

- How do you feel about goal setting? Is it something you dread, or something you look forward to?

- Have you written your goals down?

- How frequently do you review your goals?

- On a scale of 1-10, how likely are you to accomplish the goals you set?

- Do you tend to set unrealistic goals and then give up on them?

- Do you give your goals a deadline?

- Have you ever used the S.M.A.R.T. framework for goal setting? If so what were the results? If not, are you willing to give it a try?

YOUR ACTION PLAN

Honestly answer the reflection questions above either in your journal, or with your partner or a trusted friend. Then, review the S.M.A.R.T. goal examples listed above and write at least five S.M.A.R.T. financial goals of your own.

Don't worry, you don't need to work on them all at once. In fact, as you'll see in coming chapters, it's best to start small, so out of the five you write down, select one to start working on within the next 24 hours.

Finally, add a reminder to your calendar to check your weekly or monthly progress on your goal. When you complete or are close to completing the first goal, decide which goal to focus on next.

Step 3: Turn a Goal into Habits

In the previous step you created a S.M.A.R.T. goal. Great! Habits, or even a series of small habits, are the best way to master one area of your life and accomplish your S.M.A.R.T. goals. This is why you should focus on quantifying your habits by turning them into clearly identifiable actions that you complete every day, week, or month.

To get started, let's review the types of habits you can create.

Different Types of Habits

Here are three categories of habit types:

- Yes or no — Did you complete this habit for the day?
- Metric-based — A certain time, amount or quantity to reach your goal for the day.
- Project-based — Milestones where you chip away at a larger goal that has a multitude of steps. Like we mentioned before, this is what Steve calls, "Elephant habits" in his book, *Habit Stacking*.

Also, you can break down these habits into how frequently you plan on completing them. There are a few ways to do this:

Daily Habits

Lofty goals can be demotivating, so the trick is to ask yourself, "What can I do every day?" In the next chapter we'll dive deeper into creating small habits and simple goals. For now, consider what you can do **daily** to help reach one of your goals.

As you set your daily habits, keep the following two things in mind. First, make sure the daily habit leads you toward accomplishing the goal you set. Second, make sure it's realistic (the R in S.M.A.R.T). If the habits you can realistically do won't accomplish the goal, adapt the goal to be more realistic.

Examples of Daily Budgeting Habits

Here are some examples of daily budgeting habits:

- Check your credit card and checking account balances.
- If you see a credit card charge you didn't make, schedule a time to call the credit card company within 48 hours.
- Before bed, log into credit card accounts and pay off anything you purchased that day.
- Put receipts for all expenditures of the day into an envelope or section in your wallet.
- Record all expenditures of the day.
- Update your budgeting software or spreadsheet.
- Check to see if your automated budgeting software properly categorized expenditures.
- Reconcile your checkbook.
- Check your budget app before making a purchase to make sure you have available funds for the purchase.

Weekly, Monthly, and Quarterly Habits

In addition to daily budgeting habits, plan to add a few weekly, monthly, or quarterly habits to your life. These habits are helpful, but too detailed to do on a daily basis.

For example, my husband and I have a monthly financial meeting where we review our bank ac-count balances, investments, make an extra house payment, and calculate their net worth. They also discuss the progress on their big picture financial goals. This process takes between one and two hours and would be too much to do on a more frequent basis.

Another example is Steve has a weekly habit (that automatically pops up on his Todoist app) to review his credit card statements and pay all his bills.

Weekly and monthly habits are just as important as the daily actions. So here are a few additional ideas that you might want to do incorporate, though less frequently:

- Every payday allocate funds to the appropriate budget categories.

- If you use the envelope system, put cash into envelopes or count the cash you have available in each one.

- Add income into the appropriate budget category in your financial software or spreadsheet.

- Evaluate how you're progressing toward your S.M.A.R.T. goals. Are you on track? What setbacks have you encountered along the way? Do you need to make an adjustment in your daily habit?

- Check your credit card statements for recurring charges that can be eliminated.

- Call specific companies to negotiate lower prices (a great resource to learn how to do this is Ramit Sethi's free email mini-course, The Save $1,000 in 1 Week Challenge.)

- Meal plan for your family, so you're only purchasing groceries that you'll actually use.

- Comparison shop for any major purchase, like a car, electronics, and other household appliances.

There are dozens (even hundreds) of habits you can build into your day, week, or month. The trick is to identify the specific actions that will move you toward an important financial goal and then schedule them into your routine.

REFLECTION QUESTIONS

- Out of the daily habit examples listed above, which ones resonated with you most?

- Would any of the daily habit examples move you toward your S.M.A.R.T. goal?

- How can you adapt the example habits to fit your situation?

- What one habit will you commit to doing on a daily basis?

- Are there any additional budgeting habits you need to schedule weekly, monthly, or quarterly?

YOUR ACTION PLAN

Create a list of daily habit options that will help you establish the budgeting habit. Rank these habits in order of priority. Commit to doing your top choices on a daily basis. Create phone or calendar alerts to remind you to do the habit each day. (Or use one of the tools that we discuss in step #5.)

Next, make a list of weekly, monthly, and quarterly habits you want to implement. Determine when you'll do them. For instance, my husband and I have our monthly financial meeting the first Saturday morning of each month. Block out time on your calendar for these more time-consuming but less frequent actions.

Write your daily, weekly, monthly and quarterly habits along with any additional ideas you may have in your journal.

Step 4: Build a Budgeting "Habit Stack"

We're going to use the principle that Steve has developed and refined over the last five years as part of the habit stacking process. The core idea here is to build a small routine that you'll do daily (or weekly), which contains a series of small financial habits. This is what Steve calls a "**habit stack**." (For more on this concept, Steve has a lengthy blog post that goes over the step-by-step process of building a habit stack.)

As you've probably experienced, it's not easy to build new habits. You already have many tasks in your life, with an ever-increasing list of obligations, so it might seem impossible to add something new to your daily routine. It's my contention that not only do you have enough time to build a single new habit, but it's possible to add dozens of habits to your busy day without it negatively impacting your life.

All you need to do is:

1) Identify those small important actions.

2) Group them together into a routine with equally important actions.

3) Schedule a specific time each day to complete this routine.

4) Use a trigger as a reminder to complete this stack.

5) Make it super easy to get started.

In essence, the goal here is to complete the habits you know are important by stacking them on top of one another.

51

You begin with a few simple but effective habits and then build on them as this routine becomes a regular part of your day. When creating a habit stack, you want to consider a few important elements:

- Why are you choosing each action?
- What order should they go in?
- And how long do you spend on each activity?

The key to consistency is to treat a habit stack like a single action instead of a series of individual tasks. I know this seems like a small thing, but building a habit requires many elements if you want it to stick, for example:

1) Scheduling time for an activity (a block of time).
2) Identifying a trigger.
3) Planning what you'll do to complete the action.

So on and so forth.

My point here? If you treated each component of a stack as an individual action, then you'd have to create a reminder and track each behavior, which can quickly become overwhelming. However, if you treat the entire routine as just one habit, then it will be easier to remember and complete on a consistent basis. So let's talk about a six step process for building a budget-specific habit stack.

#1: Focus on one habit stack at a time.

Don't try to include too much into your already busy life because you'll probably quit when everything gets too difficult to manage. Commit to just a few simple habits that only take five to ten minutes to complete.

For instance, these can include some of the simple daily habits I mentioned before:

- Checking your credit card and checking account balances.
- Putting receipts for all expenditures of the day into an envelope or section in your wallet.
- Reconciling your checkbook.
- Checking your budget app before making a purchase to make sure you have available funds for the purchase.
- Recording all expenditures of the day.
- Updating your budgeting software or spreadsheet.

Instead of doing these tasks when you think of them, we recommend that you group them together into a budgeting stack that's scheduled for a specific time each day.

#2: Create a habit stacking trigger.

Next, we want to work on your "triggers," which are reminders that initiate the behavior.

The word *trigger* has a different meaning for many people. *Our* definition of a trigger is a cue that uses one of your five senses (sight, sound, smell, touch, or taste), which acts as a reminder to complete a specific action.

Triggers are important because most people can't remember multiple tasks without a reminder. So, a trigger can push you into taking action. For instance, many people use their alarm clocks or cell phones as a trigger to wake them up in the morning.

Here are four ways we suggest using triggers to remember the habits you'd like to build:

1) A trigger should be an existing habit. This is an action you do automatically every day, like showering, brushing your teeth, checking your phone, going to the refrigerator, or sitting down at your desk. This is important because you need to be 100% certain that you won't miss a reminder.

2) A trigger can be a specific time of day. The reminder for a habit can also happen at a specific time each day, like waking up in the morning, eating lunch, or walking through the door after work. Again, whatever you choose should be an automatic behavior.

3) A trigger should be easy to complete. If an action is challenging (even if it's something you do daily), then you decrease the effectiveness of the trigger. For instance, even if you exercise regularly, it's a mistake to use it as a trigger because you might occasionally miss a day.

4) A trigger shouldn't be a new habit. It takes anywhere from twenty-one to sixty-six days to create a permanent habit. Sometimes it's even longer for the ones that are really challenging. So, you shouldn't pick a new habit as a trigger because you're not 100% certain that it'll become a consistent action.

Here are a few examples to get the wheels turning:

- After brushing my teeth at night, I'll record all of my expenditures for the day.

- After breakfast I'll check my bank account balance.

- After getting paid, I'll log into the "You Need a Budget" (YNAB) program and record and allocate the income. (We'll talk about this tool in the next step.)

#3: Identify your common pitfalls.

Perhaps you've tried budgeting before and failed. A key step is to identify your common pitfalls to staying on a budget and then design your environment for success. For example, for my husband and I, eating out was the biggest money waster. Because of this, habits related to eating at home are crucial for us.

We all have different challenges when it comes to money. But here are a few of the most common pitfalls that was shared with us by our survey respondents:

- Forgetfulness
- Staying within the set amount for the category
- Going out with friends and not wanting to look like a penny pincher
- A child who wants and needs things
- Getting my spouse on board
- Spending money to alleviate emotional discomfort
- Impulse shopping
- Going shopping and finding good deals
- Not having money set aside for emergencies like car repairs
- Wanting to purchase before funds are available
- Allowing immediate desires to overrule long-term goals
- Spending money eating out when tired and not wanting to go home and cook
- Living paycheck to paycheck and being unable to save
- Keeping track of expenses and writing things down

- Unexpected expenses for my children like a school trip or other opportunity

- Forgetting about automatic payments and not having enough money in the account

- Unexpected large expenses that come up such as medical that I haven't saved for

- Compulsive credit card usage

#4: Design your environment for success.

Now that we've looked at some common pitfalls, let's dive into how to design your environment for success and keep you from falling prey to those pitfalls.

All you have to do is identify the challenges that you face and then create an action plan that prevents you from succumbing to these obstacles.

For instance, here are a number of strategies you can use to design your environment for success:

- Avoid taking shopping trips when bored

- Beg off requests for drinks and dinner with friends when you know they tend to go to extravagant places

- Build a social network of people who like simple activities like hiking, camping, and church

- Have frank conversations with your family where you mutually agree to tone down or eliminate the "arms race" of gift giving

- Prep much of the food for weekly meals on the weekend

- By 10:00 p.m. move meat for the next night's dinner from the freezer to fridge to thaw

- Keep staples on hand for quick, easy to prepare favorite meals
- Stick to programming like Netflix where there are no restaurant commercials
- Put credit cards in a can of water in the freezer so you can't use them without thawing
- Skip commercials and shopping channels so you're not tempted to buy unnecessary items
- Cancel paid off credit cards
- Avoid shopping malls
- Create a goal for getting out of debt in YNAB so that you'll be reminded about it every time you log in
- Budget some money each month for unexpected expenses like car repairs
- Create a list of free ways to relieve stress or reward yourself
- Instead of going out with friends that like to spend a lot of money, invite them to your place for coffee or popcorn and a Netflix movie
- Set a daily reminder on your phone or calendar to update your budget

#5: Take baby steps along the way.

Build your routine around financial habits that don't require a lot of effort (like checking your credit card and checking account balances or recording all expenditures of the day.) These are the small wins that build "emotional momentum" because they're easy to remember and complete.

Yes, they are incredibly easy tasks, but that's the point here. You want to get started with these "no-brainer" activities as they will eliminate the likelihood that you'll skip a day, even when feeling overwhelmed or busy. We recommend picking habits that are easy to complete—like anything under five minutes. Then build your stack around these simple actions.

Focus on these activities for a week or two until this stack is automatic. *Only then* should you add more habits to this routine.

Keep adding these small habits to your habit stacking routine until you have a solid thirty minutes of actions that will ultimately become a solid budgeting habit stack.

#6: Reward yourself.

Completing your habit stacking routine is an accomplishment, and it should be rewarded as such. Giving yourself a reward can be a great motivator to complete a daily routine. This can include anything, like watching your favorite TV show, eating a healthy snack, or even relaxing for a few minutes.

Really, a reward can be anything that you frequently enjoy. My only piece of advice is to avoid any reward that undermines the benefit of a specific habit.

For instance, if you've been consistently sticking to your budget for a month, the worst way to reward yourself is to go out and splurge on a high-ticket item that will derail all the hard work you've done over the past 30 days. (If you'd like more ideas, then I encourage you to read Steve's blog post that covers 155 ways to reward yourself.)

REFLECTION QUESTIONS:

- Have you thought about your triggers related to money? What often trips you up and causes you to "break your budget?"

- What's one budgeting related habit you can implement earlier in the day?

- When you've tried budgeting in the past, did you struggle with tracking your expenses?

- Up to this point, what has been your most common budgeting pitfall?

- Of the tips for designing your environment for success, which ones resonate with you the most? Can you adapt any of the ideas to better fit your personal situation?

YOUR ACTION PLAN

Now it's time to start building your first set of budgeting habits. To get started, I recommend implementing the six steps that I just detailed.

First, identify the specific habits you'd like to complete every day. Each one should take no more than five minutes to complete and the entire routine should be under 30 minutes.

Remember: The easier it is to complete these tasks, the easier it will be to turn them into permanent habits.

Next, pick a trigger for this budgeting routine. This will be a specific time of day (and often in a certain location). Furthermore, you should piggyback this trigger on top of an existing habit that you do daily—without fail.

Third, identify the specific challenges you personally face when it comes to money and budgeting. This can include a variety of things like:

forgetting to write down your expenditures, experiencing peer pressure from others to spend money, or dealing with frequent, unexpected purchases. We all have our blind spots when it comes to money, but if you identify them ahead of time, then you'll be prepared with an action plan that helps you stick to your budget.

After that, design your environment to prevent the challenges you regularly experience. This is a simple matter of knowing where you'll be tempted to break your budget and then coming up with a game plan for what you'll actually do during those moments of potential weakness. Write down each challenge and then create a detailed description of how you'll avoid this situation.

Fifth, take baby steps with your budgeting efforts. This means you should start with just a couple of financial habits that only take a few minutes each to complete. But eventually, you'll scale up and create a solid thirty-minute habit stack that helps you stick to your budget.

Finally, reward yourself with small treats when you reach important milestones. You could create a series of escalating rewards based on seven days of sticking to a budget, then two weeks, then a month, so on and so forth. If you turn budgeting into an enjoyable experience, then you'll make it that much easier to create a lasting positive, behavior change.

Step #5: Use "You Need a Budget" to Master Your Expenses

As mentioned in the introduction, 16% of our survey respondents indicated difficulty tracking spending as one of their most significant budgeting challenges. Thankfully, there are many helpful financial tracking tools. Here are some of the most popular ones:

- Spreadsheet program like Microsoft Excel
- Mint.com
- Everydollar.com
- You Need a Budget (YNAB.com)

Any of these tools work, and by all means, if you have a tool that works for you, then stick with it.

However, if you're looking for a better way to track your budget, we recommend *You Need a Budget* (commonly referred to as YNAB) for the following reasons:

- There's a free, 34-day trial, no credit card required. This gives you ample time to test the tool and see if it works for you.
- It's easily customizable.
- It's based on money you actually have rather than estimated income.
- Rather than recording things after they happen, you plan where your money will go before spending it.

- It includes a goal feature to remind you to budget for non-monthly expenditures such as quarterly car insurance payments, computer replacement, or saving up for your dream vacation. You can use YNAB to plan and track your progress on your S.M.A.R.T. goals.

- While some programs automate everything, YNAB makes you account for every dollar that comes in and goes out. Complete automation may seem ideal, but some hands-on work keeps you from checking out.

- You can have more than one budget in your account. For example, I have a budget for my business and a separate budget for my personal finances.

Now, before we move on, I want to mention a few things about YNAB and its inclusion in this book:

1) This step is completely *optional*. If you're not interested in using the YNAB program, then feel free to skip ahead to step #6.

2) Neither Steve or I have any affiliation with YNAB. The only reason we recommend it is based solely on the fact that we both feel it's the most helpful app for those who want to develop the budgeting habit.

3) This tutorial will walk you through the basics of using YNAB in conjunction with the principles found in this book. It's not intended to be an absolute guide to every feature. Instead, it's designed to give you enough of the basics, so you can quickly get started and then hit the ground running. For your convenience, we've also provided a free printable YNAB guide that's complete with screenshots. You can grab it here: www.developgoodhabits.com/budgeting-bonus

4) If you haven't already done so, be sure to complete the steps outlined in the *Getting Started with the Budgeting Habit* section of this book.

Alright, with that preamble out of the way, let's go over a nine-step process for using YNAB in conjunction with the budgeting habits principles that we discuss in this book.

Step #1: Sign up for the free, 34-day YNAB trial.

Go to www.youneedabudget.com/.

Then click on the *Try YNAB Free for 34 Days* button and fill out the form.

Note that no credit card is required to get started. (Yay!)

Simple, right?

Step #2: Create a Budget

In the upper left, click on the *My Budget* drop-down menu and then, *Budget Settings*.

Make any desired changes such as your currency type and then click on *Apply Settings*.

Step #3: Add at Least One Account

You can connect to your financial institutions electronically or manually. For the sake of this tutorial, we'll use the manual option.

Here's how to do this:

- Click on the *Add Account* button on the left.

- Click on *Skip*.

- Give your account a name (e.g. Chase checking).

- Select a BUDGET account type from one of the following options:

  - Checking

  - Savings

  - Credit Card

  - Cash

  - Line of Credit

  - PayPal

  - Merchant Account

- Fill in *Today's Balance* for that specific account. (Important! The YNAB system focuses on money you actually have, not what you expect to get next month, next week, or even tomorrow, so put the exact amount you currently have in the account.)

- Click *Save*.

- Add any additional accounts as desired.

As you add accounts and account balances, you'll see your *To Be Budgeted* amount at the top of the screen change. For example, when I added in *Chase Checking Account* and indicated that I have $1,000 in that account, the *To Be Budgeted* amount at the top showed $1,000.

Step #4: Customize Your Categories

YNAB groups items by category and then further itemizes within that *Category Group*. It comes with default categories already in place.

Let's look at the default *Category Groups* and how you might want to change them.

Monthly Priorities are things you need every single month. Included are items such as rent/mortgage, electric, and groceries. These are not optional expenses, and you spend money on them every month.

True Expenses are things that you don't spend money on every month but need to be part of your budget.

For example, Christmas and birthdays roll around just once a year. Other items such as auto maintenance and computer replacement are less predictable, but you'll likely need to spend money on them eventually. YNAB is set up in such a way that you add to your *True Expenses* categories on a regular basis, so the money is there when the need arises.

In addition to the default items listed under *True Expenses*, I like to add things I pay quarterly, bi-annually, and annually. Car insurance and property taxes are examples.

Debt Payments include things like student and auto loans.

Next is *Quality of Life Investments*. Here's where you budget for a vacation, education, fitness and so on.

Finally, you have *Fun Experiences*, which includes dining out, gaming, music, and fun money.

Deleting and Editing Categories

Not all of the default categories will apply to you. There's also a chance that some of the categories you need are missing.

For example, if your HOA pays the water bill, you can delete the *Water* category by clicking on the category, then *delete*, and then *OK*.

Alternatively, you can edit the *Water* category so that it says *HOA* instead of *Water*. You do this by clicking on the category, changing the word, "Water" to "HOA" and then clicking *OK*.

How to Add Category Groups and Categories

While the default category groups are an excellent starting point, you may want to add some custom Category Groups and categories.

For example, if you have pets, you can add a *Pets* category. Here's how: In the upper left, click on the plus sign by *Category Group*. Type in a name for the *Category Group* and click *OK*.

To add categories to the *Pets* Category Group:

- Hover over the *Pets* category until you see a plus sign.
- Click on the plus sign.
- Next, type in the name of the new category and click *OK*.

Continue this process to add additional *Category Groups* and categories.

Step #5: Set a S.M.A.R.T. Goal

The goal option in YNAB is a great way to save money toward any of the S.M.A.R.T. goals you created. For example, let's say that you set a S.M.A.R.T goal of saving $2,000 for a vacation by a set date.

You can follow these steps to add this goal to your budget in YNAB:

First, click the category where you want to create a goal. For example, for your S.M.A.R.T goal to save for a vacation, click on the *Vacation* category.

Then on the right side, you'll see a section with *Goals*. Click the plus sign next to *Create a Goal*.

You'll see there are three types of goals:

1) Target Category Balance

2) Target Category Balance by Date

3) Monthly Funding Goal

Third, select *Target Category Balance by Date* since the date component fits with the "T" in S.M.A.R.T goals.

After that, *In the Target Balance* field, type in the amount you want to save for your vacation.

Finally, select the date that you want to meet your goal, and then click on *OK*.

Now when you click on the *Vacation* category, since you haven't yet budgeted toward that goal, you'll see that you're 0% of the way toward accomplishing the goal. You'll also see how much you need to budget this month toward your vacation to stay on track with meeting your goal.

If for some reason you can't budget the recommended amount in a particular month, just budget what you can and YNAB will adjust future monthly budgets to reflect the change.

On the flip side, if you're flush with cash one month and you want to budget more than the recommended amount, YNAB automatically adjusts the recommended budget amount in future months.

Step #6: Give Every Dollar a Job

As you added your various financial accounts to YNAB, along with the account balances, the *To Be Budgeted* figure at the top of your account changed. The goal is to bring the *To be Budgeted* amount down to zero. You do this by assigning every single dollar to specific budget categories.

To budget a specific amount in a category, click on the category and then in the *Budgeted* column, type in the amount you want to budget.

For example, if your mortgage payment is $1,000 per month, you'd click on *Mortgage*, and then in the budgeted column, type in $1,000. After doing so, you'll have $1,000 available to spend on your mortgage.

When you assign money to a category, your *To Be Budgeted* amount goes down. Continue assigning dollar amounts to various categories until your *To be Budgeted* goes all the way down to zero. If you've added all the necessary budget amounts and have money left over, you can budget the remaining money to categories in future months.

If by chance you assign more money to categories than you have in *To Be Budgeted*, you'll note that it turns red. Reduce the amount budgeted in one or multiple categories to bring that number back to $0.00.

Step #7: Record Transactions

Record both money that comes in and money that goes out by clicking on the appropriate account (e.g., *Chase Checking*), and then *Add Transaction*.

Type in the *Payee* (either the person paying you or the person/company you paid) and then select the category. If you received money, place the amount in the *Inflow* field. If you paid someone, put the figure in the *Outflow* field. Finally, click on *Save*.

Step # 8: Schedule Recurring Transactions

You can set up recurring transactions such as rent that are the same amount every month.

First, click on the account that you want to pull the money from to add to the budget. In most cases, this is a checking account.

Next, click on *Add Transaction*, select the date for the next transaction and the appropriate repeat frequency.

Then type in the *Payee*, select the appropriate budget category from the drop-down menu, and put the amount in the *Outflow* field.

Finally, click on *Save*.

In the month the bill is due, you'll see an orange alert in the available column to remind you to budget for that expense.

Step #9: Move Money

Sometimes you need to make changes to your budget. YNAB refers to this as "rolling with the punches." You do this by moving money from one category to another.

For example, let's say that you get a higher-than-expected electric bill. Since you don't currently need to buy clothing, you may decide to move some money from clothing to electric.

To move money, click on the figure in the *Available* column in the category that has more budgeted than you need.

Next, enter the amount of money you want to move, and the category where you want to move the money. Then click *OK*.

Obviously, you don't want to move money from an immediate obligation category, such as rent, to a *Fun Experiences* category like gaming, unless you're sure you'll receive enough additional income to cover rent before it's due.

Digging Deeper with YNAB

You now know the basics of how to use YNAB. To learn some of the finer details such as how to break free from living paycheck to paycheck or how to handle credit cards and cash in YNAB, be sure to check out the free classes and tutorials found on the YNAB site: www.youneed-abudget.com/classes.

REFLECTION QUESTIONS:

- When you've tried budgeting in the past, did you struggle with tracking your expenses?
- Do you feel a tool like YNAB will help you stay on top of things?
- Can you commit to the daily practice of entering your expenditures into a software program like YNAB?

YOUR ACTION PLAN

First, sign up for the free 34-day YNAB trial. There's no credit card required, so no need to worry about being charged for it if you decide not to continue using it.

Next, using the information in this chapter or in this free printable tutorial (www.developgoodhabits.com/budgeting-bonus), customize YNAB to fit with your personal budget needs.

Add the S.M.A.R.T. goal you created in Step 2 of this book to YNAB. (Refer to Step 5 of the YNAB tutorial.)

Add all of your account balances to YNAB and give every dollar a job. Be sure to keep in mind the information you gleaned about your average costs for the different categories when you completed the action plan in the *Getting Started with the Budgeting Habit* chapter of this book.

Commit to using YNAB for 30 days to determine if it's the right fit for you.

Step #6: Create Accountability for Your Budgeting Goals

One of the biggest lessons that Steve has taught me is that one of the keys to successful habit development is to add *accountability* for every major goal.

It's not enough to make a personal commitment. The big things in life require a solid action plan and a support network to tap into whenever you encounter an obstacle. This is true for your career trajectory *and* your personal development. When you have someone to cheer on your successes (or kick you in the butt when you're slacking), you're less likely to give up.

There are a variety of ways to be accountable, like posting your progress on social media accounts or telling the people in your life about your new routine, but we have found that there are three strategies that get the best results.

#1: Self-accountability. You can create reminders to stick your budget using calendar alerts or Post-it Notes. You can even put alerts on your phone to remind you when to do particular activities at specific times. These apps and tools are very powerful in helping you add new habits to your daily routine.

You can also use tracking apps for *all* your habits and hold yourself accountable. I recommend these three in particular:

- StridesApp.com
- Coach.me
- HabitHub

Finally, like we just covered, one of the best tools you can use to stay on top of your finances (and stick to your budget) is to use the YNAB tool.

#2: In-person accountability. This is one of the greatest ways to form accountability for budgeting. You have a buddy that you do everything with. In the Navy SEALs, no matter what you do, you have a partner for every single mission. Since you have someone you can rely on, you feel supported and encouraged every step of the way.

The risk of choosing a buddy with the same goal as you is that if one of you stumbles, it can bring the other down also. To avoid this, build a plan for exactly what you're going to do if that buddy falls, so you don't fall with them.

Alternatively, you can have a spouse, personal friend, or an accountability partner—who just checks in to see how your process is going. You can be part of a team or a class, or even reach out to a coach. There are plenty of people who make a living by supporting and encouraging other people on the path to improving their habits and hitting their goals.

#3: Online accountability. Online accountability is a great way to check in and get quick feedback. We have that within our Facebook group: http://www.HabitsGroup.com.

You can also find online accountability partners and coaches. We've done our best to provide an environment where people can reach out, communicate and give each other online support. If you have questions about shifting your goals or what to do if you stumble, having an online community can make a big difference and help you stay the course.

Be Honest About Your Failures

Sticking to a budget is a war, not a battle. It's a process that you develop over time, not in a moment. This means you will have some slipups and tough days. Even if you fail to track your expenses for a few days, this doesn't mean that you're a failure. Instead, it's a minor hiccup in your journey toward building a positive money habit.

I say all this as a reminder that an accountability buddy is not there to judge you but to *support you*. That's why it's important to be honest with this person when you have a slipup. This doesn't mean you're a failure. Instead, you're showing a dedication to the accountability process by admitting to those days when you're not sticking to your budget.

Never Break the Chain

The book, *The One Thing* tells the story of Jerry Seinfeld's "don't break the chain" approach that led to his success as a comedian. As the story goes, before Seinfeld became a household name, he made a commitment to write jokes **every** day. To keep himself accountable, he put a huge annual calendar on his wall and put a red X across every day that he wrote a joke. The goal is to not break the chain.

As Seinfeld said, "Just keep at it and the chain will grow longer every day. You'll like seeing the chain, especially when you get a few weeks under your belt. Your only job is to not break the chain. **Don't break the chain.**"

This can be a very powerful approach for you too. Put a monthly calendar on the wall, and every time you have a success, draw a big X on the day when it's completed. Build a chain of success. You can also use Strides, Coach.me, or HabitHub to track your success; they use the same chain idea.

Our main goal is to recognize that even when we have a day that's less than perfect, we want to maintain that chain of positive action. We don't want to have a complete break. You might have a day where you don't do everything you planned for sticking to a budget. But even if you still spend a few minutes reviewing your budget, then you can consider that a successful day.

Reward Important Milestones

New habits don't have to be boring. Seeing your "chain" getting longer in and of itself can be exciting. On top of that, take the time to celebrate the successful completion of your goals. The reward you pick is up to you, but it's important to celebrate those big moments along the way.

Keep in mind that your reward doesn't have to break the bank. You could check out a new movie, enjoy a night out with your significant other, or simply do something you love.

Again: Just make sure that your reward doesn't conflict with your goal. For example, if your goal is to get out of debt, don't celebrate by going out to a fancy dinner and charging it on your credit card!

Option #1: Create funding goals in YNAB for each of the rewards you plan.

For instance, if you plan to go out to dinner after 21 consecutive days of checking your bank balance, budget the appropriate amount for dinner out so the money's there when you meet that milestone.

Monthly funding or target-date goals are especially important for bigger milestones that may include bigger, more expensive rewards. Save consistently, and then enjoy the reward guilt free!

Option #2: Set up a token economy.

In the article *How to Beat Procrastination by Creating a "Token Economy,"* blogger Patrik Edblad shares the following tips for creating a token economy:

- Create specific and measurable daily quotas.

- Get some type of token to award yourself. For example, poker chips, pennies, beads, or some other random thing you have laying around the house.

- Every time you complete the specific task, put a token into a container.

- Use your tokens to "buy" rewards. For instance, you may reward yourself with dinner out after you have 21 tokens, or splurge on a spa day when you have 90 tokens.

Option #3: Create a visual reminder of your success.

The YouTuber, Homespun Wife, shares about her "Blue Bottle of Happiness" on this video. Every time she and her husband paid off a credit card, they cut it up and put it into a blue, decorative bottle. The bottle is now full of cut up credit cards and serves as a reminder and trophy of their victory over debt.

If you don't have credit card debt but still want a visual reminder of your budgeting habit success journey, you may opt to add a smooth stone, bead, or shiny penny to a clear vase or jar every day you complete a mini habit. Display your "trophy" where you'll see it every day as a reminder of how far you've progressed on your financial journey.

Option #4: Give yourself a talking to.

James Clear often tells himself at the end of a workout, "That was a good day" or "Good job. You made progress today." If you feel like it, you can tell yourself, "Victory!" or "Success" each time you do a new habit.

REFLECTION QUESTIONS:

- Which of the three types of accountability (self, online, in person) have you tried? What worked best for you? If you haven't tried any, which type do you feel would work best for you?

- What are some of the biggest challenges you've experienced with accountability?

- How have you personally benefited from accountability?

- Have you ever shared personal information for accountability purposes on a blog or YouTube channel?

- What habit can you realistically do on a daily basis to keep from breaking the chain?

- What visual reminders or rewards will you create to keep your motivation level high?

YOUR ACTION PLAN

Select one of the apps mentioned earlier in this chapter to track the one daily habit you decided to focus on in Step 3. See how long you can go without breaking the chain!

Next, set up either in person or online accountability. You can either join a budget-specific group, or join the Develop Good Habits Facebook group and share your goals so we can hold you accountable.

Create a milestone such as checking your bank balance daily for 30 days, and then come up with a way to celebrate when you reach the milestone. Be sure that the way you decide to celebrate doesn't conflict with your financial goals.

Finally, set up a token system or some other form of visual accountability such as a wall calendar or your own blue bottle of happiness.

Step #7: Do a Weekly Review

To stay on track and keep small setbacks from becoming deeply ingrained negative habits, plan to spend 20—30 minutes once a week reviewing all your habits and goals. During your weekly review, start by celebrating wins—both big and small.

Next, reflect on any mistakes that you've made. Look for patterns to identify obstacles to your success. For instance, upon reflection you may realize that you blow your budget every time you get together with your sister or a particular friend. Or perhaps you pick up fast food every time your child has a little league baseball game. Or you may also find that the root cause of your setbacks is that you've set too big of a goal.

Third, as you go through the weekly review process, you'll continually find new triggers. Being vigilant and working this plan will help you isolate, analyze, and overcome, so you can either replace those triggers with triggers for positive habits or remove those triggers from your life. If the same mistakes keep happening, ask yourself why. Is the goal too big? Are there other obstacles?

At the end of this weekly review, ask yourself three questions and write down the answers in your journal:

- What went right?
- What went wrong?
- How can I plan for next week?

As an example, every week, I check the HabitHub app on my phone for the hard facts about how the week went. I then set a timer and spend 30 minutes freewriting about the events of the week, both good and bad. As I write, I'll often gain clarity about the issues at the root of my struggles. Finally, I'll devise a plan for overcoming those obstacles the next week, and if needed, adjust my goals.

REFLECTION QUESTIONS

- What is your current process for reviewing your habits and goals.

- If you already do a weekly review, what is your process? Is the process working for you?

- Are there others such as a spouse or accountability partner you should involve in the review? If so, who are they and what role will they play?

YOUR ACTION PLAN

The first actions for this step are to decide what to review weekly, what questions to ask yourself in your review, the tools you'll use for your review, and then what you'll do as a result of the review.

For instance, you may opt to review just your budget in YNAB, ask yourself how you did in your budget that week, and then adapt your budget or your spending plans for the coming week based on what you found in your review.

Or you may choose to use your habit tracking app such as HabitHub to look at the hard facts when it comes to your consistency, and if things didn't go well, ask yourself what hindered you from doing better and what you need to do in the coming week to up your level of consistency.

Like Steve, you may have a set of questions to ask yourself and record the answers in Evernote or your journal.

In light of the above, write the following in your journal:

- What habits or goals you'll review weekly
- What questions to ask yourself in the review
- The tools you'll use for your review
- The types of action steps you'll take in the coming week as a result of the review

By the way, be sure to set a time for your weekly review and add it to your calendar. Be committed to the review like you would any other appointment. If something comes up for the same time as your review that you simply must do, rather than skipping the review, schedule it for another time.

Step #8: Plan for Obstacles

Even if you've designed your environment for success, every habit, including budgeting, has obstacles. The best way to overcome them is to anticipate the obstacles ahead of time and have an action plan ready.

Here are some common budgeting obstacles that our survey respondents shared, along with specific solutions for overcoming them.

#1: Unexpected Expenses

Imagine that everything's humming along with your budget. You've given every dollar a job. You feel good about it—until you get a bill for something like car insurance that you pay once a year, or until you wake up freezing because the furnace went out. You look at your budget and because you didn't expect those expenses, you don't have the money, period. Not knowing what else to do, you resort to pulling out a credit card, which only puts you deeper in debt.

The best way to deal with unexpected expenses is to expect them and budget for them in advance. For things that bill regularly, but less frequently than monthly, set up a *Target Category Balance* by Date goal in YNAB.

For instance, if your annual car insurance payment of $1,588 is due June of each year, set up a goal to save up that amount by June. YNAB then automatically calculates how much you need to add to your budget each month, so the money is there when the payment is due.

It's not as easy with things such as car repairs or the furnace going out because you have no idea when those things will happen or how much they'll cost. The best way to prepare is to build up a general emergency fund to handle these unexpected expenses or add to your car repair or household maintenance budget on a monthly basis.

#2: Impulse Buys

You're standing in the checkout line at the grocery store, and a compelling magazine headline grabs your attention. "It's less than $10," you reason, so you buy it, even though it's not in your budget. That's a small purchase, but all those small impulse buys add up. Worse, not all impulse buys are small.

Here are a variety of simple strategies you can use to curb those impulse buys:

- Use the cash envelope system for everything other than regular monthly bills. While you can still succumb to impulse buys with cash, you feel it more when you pull the money out of the envelope. You also clearly see how much money you have left in the envelope and the impact of the "little" purchase. Plus, when you have nothing but cash in your wallet, there's a hard limit on how much you can spend.

- Use a shopping list and commit to sticking to it. If it's not on the list, put it down and walk away.

- Unsubscribe from email lists that pitch tempting products or services.

- Avoid shopping channels or network television with commercials.

- To keep from feeling deprived, rather than telling yourself, "I can't buy it" say, "I'll buy it tomorrow." Keep telling yourself that until you either work it into your budget or decide you no longer want to purchase the item.

- Leave your credit cards at home. Even better, freeze your credit cards in a coffee can filled with water so that it takes time and effort to access them.

- Avoid shopping with friends that are big spenders.

#3: Friends & Family

Speaking of friends, a lot of our survey respondents mentioned going out with friends as a big hindrance to their budget. Other's indicated that expenses related to their children such as field trips, cheerleading outfits and other random kid-related expenses threw them off. In addition to that, many find family gift giving to be a budget buster.

For the unexpected expenses for your children, refer back to number one. Add a "kids" or "school expenses" category to your budget and regularly set aside money for those irregular but important expenditures.

If you find the expenses are higher than you can realistically budget for, explain the situation to your children and get their input on what things matter most and then budget for those things.

If you have teens, let them know what you're willing to cover and what they'll need to earn on their own. You may also provide them with a set amount of spending money each month for activities, clothing, and other items and teach them how to budget that money.

Be up front with your friends and family about your budgeting habit journey to help set expectations about changes in your spending habits.

#4: Spouses

While we mentioned family in the last point, so many of our readers indicated that their spouses were unwilling to cooperate, we decided this deserved a separate point, with three different strategies you can use to communicate with your spouse.

The first strategy we recommend is to initiate "productive conflict."

Most of us avoid conflict, even when we want a specific outcome. We may give in too quickly, failing to meet our own needs or fall short of coming up with helpful solutions. On the flip side, we may dig in our heels and try to persuade our spouse that our belief is the right one.

To improve communication as couples, we need to get better at initiating a productive conflict. What does that mean? It means understanding how to approach and resolve conflicts in ways that generate helpful solutions while protecting the relationship.

A productive conflict doesn't mean just being "nicer" about fighting. Rather, it means, having an intentional and healthy process for working through differences. And this is where negotiation becomes so important.

Negotiating well means using a process for creating better solutions—one that meets each partner's most important needs and preferences.

Before you begin the conversation, be sure to review the nine steps outlined here to keep you on track.

1) Choose the right time for a discussion.

Make sure you're both rested, in a good frame of mind, and unlikely to be interrupted.

2) Start with constructive language.

If you begin with something like, "I'd like to discuss the way you manage our money," it sounds like a criticism, as the problem appears to be with your partner.

Instead try something like, "I'd like to see if we can agree on some rules for our budget and money management." This is a more constructive way of opening the conversation by naming a positive goal rather than implying a problem with your partner.

3) Create mutual ground rules.

There are things you or your partner can say or do that will immediately get the conversation off to a bad start. For example, using the words "always" and "never" can make your partner bristle.

4) Listen and validate first.

Remember that letting your partner feel heard and understood is a powerful way to help him or her feel safe and willing to be more generous and flexible in negotiation and compromise.

5) Brainstorm several options.

Before you propose a solution, engage in a short period of brainstorming, where you both present several solutions without criticizing one another.

Once you have many possibilities on the table, you may find that combining several of them is easily agreeable to both of you.

6) Seek outside support from others.

A trusted friend or family member can help you clarify and articulate what is really bothering you and what your goals are. They can help you brainstorm a constructive way to open the conversation, as well as think of questions to ask and ways to talk about your fears.

7) Reframe criticism as complaint.

As relationship expert John Gottman has discovered, there is an important difference between a complaint and criticism. Complaint points to a behavior as the problem, where criticism implies a quality or trait of your partner is the problem.

8) Use the phrase, "Is there anything else?"

Allowing the real issue to emerge at the beginning of a discussion can save a lot of time and emotional energy.

9) Learn and practice repair moves.

Repair moves are words or actions that can lessen the tension if the conversation begins to get heated. Four powerful repair moves include humor, reminiscing about a past happy or fun time together, apologizing for your part in the problem, and using loving touch and affection.

Another strategy we recommend is to develop the "active listening" habit with your partner.

Active listening is not an easy habit to master, mainly because most of us are more motivated to talk than listen. It's more challenging than basic listening because active listening requires you to be fully present. It is often needed during uncomfortable times If you wish to be more of an active listener with your partner, you must be willing to do the following:

- Allow your partner to dominate the conversation and determine the topic to be discussed.
- Remain completely attentive to what he or she is saying.

- Avoid interrupting, even when you have something important to add.

- Ask open-ended questions that invite more from your partner (if he or she wants that).

- Avoid coming to premature conclusions or offering solutions.

- Repeat back to your partner what you heard once he or she is done speaking.

To dig deeper into these topics, be sure to check out the book, *Mindful Relationship Habits* that Steve co-authored with Barrie Davenport.

The final strategy we recommend is to put your partner in charge of their favorite spending categories.

My daughter, Haley is a spender. My son-in-law, Anthony is a saver. He came up with a great solution to this problem. He handles 95% of the budget, including vital things such as housing, food, and investments. Haley handles just one budget category—the fun budget. Having complete control of this one aspect of their finances gives her the freedom to blow money on things she enjoys without compromising their budget as a whole.

If your partner tends to spend more than budgeted even in those areas, suggest using the cash envelope system for those specific budget categories.

#5: Irregular Income

If you're in commission-based sales or self-employed, you likely have irregular income. Some months you make a lot, other months much less. This makes budgeting difficult since you never know how much money will come in each month.

The best way to deal with an irregular income is to calculate your average income over the past several months. From there, give yourself a set monthly salary that is a little less than your average income. Each month regardless of how much or little you make, pay yourself by transferring your pre-determined salary into your checking account.

When you handle your money this way, you won't feel overly rich and blow money during the months when you make a killing, and stress when you have lean months. Of course, if you have several lean months in a row, you may need to adapt your salary to fit your current reality.

#6: Eating Out

It's hard to break the temptation to eat out, particularly if you do it habitually. The problem is, money spent eating out quickly adds up and can completely blow your budget. Here are a few ways to reduce the amount of money you spend eating out.

- Create a weekly meal plan focused on family favorites that are easy to prepare.
- Once a week, do as much prep work as you can, such as cutting up vegetables ahead of time.
- Prepare a double batch of a main dish and freeze one to use in the future.
- Before bed, move meat for the next night's dinner from the freezer to fridge to thaw.
- Keep staples on hand for quick, easy to prepare meals.
- Order shelf stable meal kits from a company like Takeout Kit to satisfy your craving for restaurant-style ethnic food.

Plan for Big Obstacles

Some of the obstacles mentioned above are small, but have a big impact since they happen frequently. Less common are big obstacles such as major health issues or job loss. While substantial life changes that impact a budget happen much less frequently, it's good to have a plan, just in case.

If One of Us Lost Our Job...

When my husband and I set out to purchase a home, we did what most people do—got prequalified for a loan. I immediately began to look at homes that, according to the bank, we could afford. My husband, however, kept showing me a home he found online that was about half of the prequalified amount. I wasn't at all interested, but finally agreed to go see it, mostly so he'd stop bugging me.

The moment we walked into the home, I thought, "If one of us lost our job, we could still afford this house payment." In spite of the fact that we both had what appeared to be secure jobs, that thought changed my perspective, and I immediately fell in love with the house.

Fast forward a year later, when my husband walked through the door with a box of his personal items and a dejected look on his face. When he told me that he lost his job, I remembered my thought the first time I stepped foot in our home, and I knew we would be okay.

The key to preparing for big financial obstacles is to voluntarily live on less now, rather than waiting until you have no choice. Perhaps you'll downsize your house, buy a less expensive car, or cut back on nice but unnecessary things, like eating out. Since people with little or no debt can live on less, do whatever it takes to pay off debt, and pay cash for everything going forward.

Once you make these changes, you'll find you have a lot of money leftover at the end of the month. Funnel that extra money into the emergency fund category in YNAB, and as the balance grows, you'll have less anxiety about the big financial obstacles that are beyond your control.

When You Mess Up...

In spite of your best intentions, you may completely blow your budget. Maybe you go on vacation and spend twice as much as you'd planned. Or perhaps you go through a very stressful time at work or in your personal life and simply stop budgeting for a couple of months.

These times are discouraging, but don't have to be fatal. Take a deep breath—and revisit your purpose. Remind yourself why you want to stick with a budget. While it's important to be honest with yourself about your failure, don't beat yourself up. Tomorrow is a new day, and it's never too late for a fresh start.

REFLECTION QUESTIONS

- Out of the obstacles listed in this chapter, which one resonated the most with you?

- What have you tried up to this point to deal with the obstacle? What has and hasn't worked?

- In what ways have you allowed the opinions of others to impact your finances in a negative way?

- How often do you make purchases to impress or gain the approval of others? Are you willing to let go of trying to impress others in order to get your financial house in order?

YOUR ACTION PLAN

First, grab your journal and write the answers to each of the questions above.

Next, create your own personal list of tactics you can use to overcome each of your biggest obstacles. For example, if impulse buys are your biggest struggle and as a result you are deeply in debt, commit to taking two actions from the list we provided, such as freezing your credit cards in a can of water and switching to the cash envelope system.

If your challenges center around other people such as friends or your spouse, schedule a time to talk with them about the changes you're making and ask for their help. Be sure to frame the conversation in such a way that you don't point fingers. Stand your ground in a calm, polite, and affirming way.

Think for a moment about what you'd do if you have a big financial setback, such as a job loss. How would you make it work? What adjustments could you make to stretch your dollars? Are there any changes you can make now to prepare for a big financial crisis?

As always, don't make too many drastic changes at once. Commit to one or two actions that address your current biggest obstacle.

Step #9: Maximize Those "Slivers of Time"

Even if you only have a few minutes to work on your budget, we recommend that you still do something. The idea here is to use those "short slivers of time."

As discussed by Suzanne Perez Tobias, in addition to any daily habits you develop, you can also maximize short slivers of time to make steady progress with your goals. Yes, it's true that you won't get the same impact in little bits of time that you do when devoting larger blocks of time, but something is better than nothing, right?

Here are some examples of how to use small time increments to stay on top of your budget:

- Write down expenditures as they occur.
- Check your bank balance or your budget app on your phone before making a purchase.
- Add the Amazon Kindle app and load it up with personal finance books to read whenever you have a few spare minutes.
- Review your goals and make sure your actions are reflecting these outcomes.
- Check all your financial statements to make sure there are no unauthorized charges.

It's easy to discount those spare moments of time you have throughout the day. We often think it's not possible to accomplish anything important in just five or ten minutes. However, if you commit yourself to taking a little bit of action in the time that you do have, then you can use that to maximize the impact on your budgeting efforts.

REFLECTION QUESTIONS

- What do you typically do when you're stuck sitting around waiting for something or someone?
- What finance-related tasks can you accomplish in less than five minutes?
- Are there any finance books you'd like to read but don't feel you have time for?
- What apps or programs can you add to your phone in order to maximize those spare moments you have throughout the day?

YOUR ACTION PLAN

Over the next week, be mindful of wasted moments where you're sitting around doing nothing and make note of them in your journal. Some examples are waiting for your friend to meet you at the gym, sitting at the doctor's office, or waiting to pick your kids up from school. Each of those examples happen outside the home, but also consider the wasted bits of time at home as well, like waiting for the oven to preheat or the family to come to the dinner table.

The point is to train yourself to recognize little slivers of time so that they don't pass you by without notice. Jot down those things as they occur. Challenge yourself to come up with at least ten things over the course of the next week.

Next, divide that list into things that happen regularly vs. infrequently. For instance, you may sit in your car waiting to pick up your kids from school every Monday through Friday, but only go to the doctor or dentist once a quarter.

After dividing the list, create a simple list of statements for each of those slivers of time. For instance, "If I'm waiting to pick up my kids from school, I'll enter each of my expenditures for the day in YNAB."

Step #10: Six Ways to Scale Up Your Budgeting Efforts

If you want to supercharge your progress toward your financial goals, then you can scale up with personal challenges.

Here are six ideas to get you started.

#1. Establish a Temporary Spending Freeze

Whether you feel overwhelmed by debt or you are tired of how long it's taking to save toward a big financial goal such as a new car— to accelerate your efforts—enact a spending freeze in one or more categories.

For instance, in her video The Truth About Money: Tackling HUGE CREDIT CARD DEBT, YouTuber Homespun Wife tells the story of how when she and her husband were trying to get out of debt, they made a commitment not to spend **any** money on clothing —including little things like socks and underwear—for an entire year.

Others go as far as spending money on nothing but essentials such as food, utilities and rent for an entire year.

If either of these examples seem too extreme to you, try a short spending freeze. For instance, if you buy coffee on the way to work every morning, commit to skipping it for a week.

Regardless of how long or short your spending freeze lasts, apply the saved money toward a goal, such as paying off credit cards or saving for a new car.

#2. Gradually Decrease Spending

If you're not quite ready for a spending freeze, you may opt to gradually decrease your spending. For instance, if you currently spend $600 per month eating out, this month commit to spending only $550, then next month $500, and the next month $450. Continue this process until you hit a point that stretches you but is sustainable.

#3. Gradually Increase Savings or Investing

Some people don't put money into savings or investment accounts because they feel they can't afford to. There could be some truth to that, particularly if your bills are high and your income is low. But even if you feel like you can't afford to save or invest, make a small commitment such as $5 per week—or even a month if needed. The following week or month increase that amount to $6, then $7, then $8, and so on. As you continue that process, it will become clear when you've hit your limit. Maintain that level of investing from there on out until you feel ready to stretch yourself again.

#4. Embark on an Income-Producing Challenge

Author Canna Campbell shares how she saved $32,000 in a year using her $1,000 Project approach. Rather than focusing on a big and over-whelming goal such as saving $32,000, she looked for ways to bring in extra cash. Each time she saved up $1,000, she invested that money in blue chip stocks.

The key is to break a big goal into smaller chunks, find ways to bring in extra money, and each time you save up a set amount of money, apply it to your big goal. Many people make extra money selling things from around the house in yard sales, on eBay or Craigslist, or taking on a seasonal job.

If you get stuck, then I recommend creating income through a strategy that's commonly known as a "side hustle," which is a part-time activity that *could* turn into a full-time income.

The downside of side hustling *isn't* a lack of opportunities. In fact, the problem is there are too many choices here, which makes it hard to pick one and stick with it. That's why you need to find a side hustle that fits within your time and monetary restrictions.

While there are countless resources you can use to research a side hustle, the best starting point is an extensive blog post on Nick Loper's Side Hustle Nation and his book *Buy Buttons*. Both provide a great overview of the different income-generating opportunities and what you need to do to create a similar business.

#5. Make a Game of It

Here are two financial games to play if you want to get one of your impulse spending areas under control.

Double or Nothing

First, pick an unnecessary spending category that you want to cut back on such as stopping at Starbucks every day on the way to work. Next, choose something you want to invest more money into such as paying off debt or investing in your retirement fund.

For a set period of time such as a week, month, or 90 days, commit to putting the same amount of money you spend on the unnecessary category into paying off debt or adding to savings.

For instance, using the coffee example, every time you spend $7 on coffee, you have to also deposit an extra $7 into your savings account. This means that every $7 cup of coffee ends up costing you $14. If you apply this to eating out, every $50 dinner ends up costing you $100, and so on. This increased cost makes you think twice about spending money unnecessarily, and even if you do spend it, half of your total cost moves you closer to one of your financial goals.

Do This Not That

Look for extra money by replacing expensive spending options with less expensive alternatives. Then use the money you save toward one of your financial goals.

For instance, if you're tempted to order a pizza, instead make a simple meal at home. If you want to go to a movie, instead stay home and watch one on Netflix or Vudu. If you see a new outfit you want at the mall, go to the thrift store and see if you can find something comparable. Next, calculate your savings and then apply the saved money to your credit card or one of your goals in YNAB.

#6. Age Your Money

If you've started using YNAB, you may have noticed that after you've recorded ten transactions, in the upper right there's an "age of money" figure. If you spend money as soon as it comes in, you're living paycheck to paycheck and your age of money is low. To break the paycheck to paycheck cycle, hold on to your money as long as possible. As you do, your age of money goes up.

When most people start using YNAB, their *Age of Money* is a couple of days or less. Set a goal of increasing that to 30 days. For most people this process takes a few months, so celebrate some smaller milestones such as 7, 14 and 21 days along the way.

REFLECTION QUESTIONS

- Are you discouraged by how much debt you have or how little money you have in savings?
- Do you feel that it's near impossible to save enough up for a down payment on a home or for retirement?
- What other financial dreams do you have that feel out of reach?
- Which of the ideas for scaling up with personal challenges resonated with you the most?
- How can implementing even one of the ideas impact your progress on getting out of debt or saving up for one of your financial dreams?

YOUR ACTION PLAN

It's time to supercharge your progress toward your financial goals, and you're going to do it by implementing at least one of the personal challenges presented in this chapter.

Let's start by getting out your journal and being honest about any discouragement you may feel in the area of finances.

Next, take a look at the list of ideas in this chapter and pick one to implement this week. For instance, maybe you're not ready to go without buying clothing for the entire year, but you are willing to skip eating out for the entire week.

Calculate how much money you'll save by this one change, and determine what you'll do with the money saved. For instance, you may determine that you'll save $100 this week by not eating out and with the money you save you'll pay $100 extra on your credit card debt, or put $100 into savings.

Put a reminder on your calendar for next week to consider the same or a new challenge for the coming week. Consider adding this to your weekly financial review. Some weeks you may feel too busy or stressed to embark on one of these challenges, and that's fine. The key is to keep these money-saving challenges top of mind and implement them as often as possible.

Next, create your own income-producing challenge such as the $1,000 Project. Start off by dreaming about what you could do with an extra $200, $500, $1000 or more per month. Would you travel the world? Save for a down payment on a home? Remodel your kitchen? Catch up on your retirement savings? Pay off all credit card debt?

Now brainstorm a list of side hustle options you could try to bring in extra money. If you're not very entrepreneurial, consider seasonal jobs such as working in a retail store during the holiday season, working for the local parks service during the summer, or delivering newspapers or pizzas throughout the year. If the thought of extra work overwhelms you, relieve that stress by committing to a shorter period of time.

Be sure to keep track of the money you save, extra money you make, and the resulting progress toward your big-picture dreams.

Resources for Mastering Your Finances

We want to help you dive deep into the area of personal finance. The best way to go about that is to totally immerse yourself in the topic. Read books and blogs, listen to podcasts, watch YouTube videos and if you really want to dive deep, take a few online courses.

If this feels like too much work, rest assured that it's worth it.

Why?

Because you move toward whatever you focus on. It's like a magnet.

If you focus on the latest gadgets, fashions, or how good a cheeseburger tastes, you'll move that direction, and so will your money. At the end of the month, you'll wonder why your bank account is empty, or even worse, overdrawn.

In contrast, as you immerse yourself in personal finance, you'll find that your entire attitude toward money changes. As your attitude changes, so will your actions. You'll move from spending money carelessly to spending it intentionally, and before you know it, your entire financial situation will dramatically improve.

To help you get started, here is an extensive list of books, podcasts, blogs, videos, courses and tools you can use to master your finances. With just a small financial investment (and a little bit of your free time), you can get a world-class education on mastering your finances.

Books

- *The Total Money Makeover* by Dave Ramsey
- *Retire Inspired* by Chris Hogan
- *You Need a Budget* by Jesse Mecham
- *Living Well, Spending Less* by Ruth Soukup

Podcasts

- Listen, Money Matters
- Stacking Benjamins
- The Dave Ramsey Show
- You Need a Budget
- Part-Time Money
- Money for the Rest of Us
- Firedrill Podcast
- Marriage, Kids and Money
- Millennial Money Minutes
- Money Girl's Quick and Dirty Tips
- Cash Flow Diary
- Good Financial Cents
- So Money
- The Side Hustle Show
- Feed the Pig
- Teach Me How To Money

Blogs

- Mr. Money Mustache
- Get Rich Slowly
- Money Girl's Quick and Dirty Tips
- Well Kept Wallet
- Money Under 30
- Frugalwoods
- Afford Anything
- The Penny Hoarder
- Man Vs. Debt
- Money Saving Mom
- Budgets Are Sexy
- Disease Called Debt
- Frugal Rules
- Good Financial Cents
- 20 Something Finance
- Financial Samurai
- Daily Worth
- The Centsible Life
- Couple Money
- Punch Debt in the Face
- Jessi Fearon

YouTube Channels

- TruFinancials
- Freedom in a Budget
- Our Life On a Budget
- The Dave Ramsey Show
- Common Cents Mike
- Plenteouz of Money
- His and Her Money
- Dollar Dude
- Budget Girl
- Frugal Green Girl

Courses

- Finance Training and Tutorials on Lynda.com
- How to Build a Budget and Start Saving Money

Calculators

- Practical Money Skills
- Compound Interest Calculator

REFLECTION QUESTIONS

- Is this the first budgeting book you've ever read?
- What else have you done to learn about personal finance?
- Can you see how becoming an expert in personal finance will encourage you to stick with your budget when temptations arise?

- Is there any critical piece of knowledge or information you feel was missing from this book?

- Are you ready to go out and look at these other resources to continue growing and learning about how to finally get a handle on your finances?

YOUR ACTION PLAN

I want you to go through each of these links. If it's not easy for you to click all these, we have a dedicated personal finance page, and every single link and book we reference is available here: www.developgoodhabits.com/budgetingnotes

For this activity, you're going to check out each of these resources and simply find the ones that resonate with you. Take the information you learned from these sources and delve deeper. Add notes into your journal, Evernote or OneNote to develop your own personal finance encyclopedia.

Conclusion

I know it might seem impossible to make a big financial dream come true. So before we close things out, I'd like to share the story of YouTuber Denis Trufin, of TruFinancials, who managed to pay cash for a home at the age of 22.

Here's a summary of his story that he shares in his video, How I bought my first home debt free at 22.

According to Denis, a three-pronged approach including hard work, good timing, and luck—all played a part in his accomplishment.

First, at the age of 18, he put in the time and effort at his job to demonstrate his capabilities. This led to a promotion. With the raise, he decided to save toward paying cash for a home. This seemed far-fetched, even to him, since he was so young.

As he budgeted, he found that he was overspending small amounts in small categories. He said that some people feel justified in spending things that cost just a few dollars, but when he stopped spending money on those items, he discovered how much those small things impacted his budget.

Finally, he found a beaten-down home that was going for a very low price. It was so low he felt he could make a cash offer for lower than the asking price. Since his offer was cash, it was more attractive than the higher non-cash offers on the home.

While luck and timing (a housing crisis) played a part, his hard work of saving every dollar possible positioned him to take advantage of a good opportunity.

I'll leave you with two quotes that Denis shared in his video:

- "The more hard work you put in, the more luck comes toward you."
- "Be intentional with your money. It seems to listen better."

The lesson here is that if you're willing to fully commit to the budgeting habit, then this practice will pay dividends for many years to come!

We'd like to congratulate you on reaching the end of this book. Now your real financial freedom journey begins!

While it may be tempting to embark on this journey alone, as we mentioned in Step 5, accountability increases the odds of sticking with something, and ultimately leads to greater success.

In fact, as an African proverb states, "If you want to go fast, go alone. If you want to go far, go together." While it's tempting to go fast, we know that going far is the key to financial success. With that in mind, join our Facebook group at HabitsGroup.com. Then share your journey toward financial freedom with the group.

Your 30-Day Plan

While budgeting is a life-long habit, we want you to start the journey by following this 30-day plan.

First, review the action steps we provided at the end of each chapter. For your convenience, we created a free printable PDF which you can get here: www.developgoodhabits.com/budgeting-bonus

Next, set your first 30-day goal and post it in the group. An example of a 30-day goal is, "Set up my budget in YNAB."

Third, post your goal along with the date, in the Facebook group.

Then, break your goal down into 30 daily goals. For example, if your 30-day goal is to set up your budget in YNAB, before doing so, you need to take the first steps of calculating your income and expenses, categorizing your expenses, determining how much you need in each category, and signing up for the 34-day YNAB trial. Divide those bigger tasks into small, daily tasks that result in accomplishing your goal in the next 30 days.

After that, break each of your daily goals into tiny tasks. "Download the budget spreadsheet" is an example of a tiny task.

Choose a few small habits, such as checking your bank balance daily, or writing down your expenditures for at least the next seven days.

Finally, write down your #1 obstacle when it comes to budgeting, and then take one step to overcome that obstacle. For instance, if impulsive credit card use is your #1 obstacle, put your credit cards in a can of water in the freezer so you can't use them without thawing.

Finally, as we bring this book to a close we want to remind you that developing the budgeting habit is a journey. Your initial budget likely won't be perfect, and it will take time before you see big results. But we promise if you follow the step-by-step plan we've provided in this book, your financial future will be brighter than your current reality.

Thank you so much for reading.

We can't wait to see the difference that the budgeting habit makes in your life.

Cheers,
Rebecca Livermore & S.J. Scott

One Last Reminder...

We've covered a wealth of information in this book, but that doesn't mean your budgeting efforts should end here. In fact, we've created two exclusive bonuses that will help you take action on what you've learned in *The Budgeting Habit*.

First you will get access to a tracking spreadsheet you can use to track all your spending. And second, you will get a copy of the and visual walkthrough of the "You Need a Budget" software program. You can access both in the link below:

So, if you're interested in expanding on what you've learned in this book, then click this link and grab these bonuses today:

www.developgoodhabits.com/budgeting-bonus

Thank You!

Before you go, we'd like to say thank you for purchasing our book.

You could have picked from dozens of books on habit development, but you took a chance and chose this one.

So, big thanks for downloading this book and reading all the way to the end.

Now we'd like to ask for a small favor. **Could you please take a minute or two and leave a review for this book on Amazon?**

This feedback will help us continue to write the kind of Kindle books that help you get results. And if you loved it, please let us know.

More Books by Rebecca

Blogging

- *Blogger's Quick Guide to Starting Your First WordPress Blog*
- *Blogger's Quick Guide to Writing Rituals and Routines*
- *Blogger's Quick Guide to Blog Post Ideas*
- *Blogger's Quick Guide to Working with a Team*
- *Blogging for Authors*
- *Content Repurposing Made Easy*

Christian Living

- *Godly Freedom: Devotional Readings from 1 Corinthians*
- *By the Will of God: Devotional Readings from 2 Corinthians*
- *Faith that Forgives: Devotional Readings from Philemon*
- *A Fresh Start with Jesus: Embracing the God of Second Chances*

India Travel

- *Rickshaws, Rajas and Roti*

Co-Written with Steve Scott

- *The Daily Entrepreneur*
- *Level Up Your Day*
- *Confident You*

More Books by Steve

- *The Anti-Procrastination Habit: A Simple Guide to Mastering Difficult Tasks*
- *10-Minute Mindfulness: 71 Habits for Living in the Present Moment*
- *Habit Stacking: 127 Small Changes to Improve Your Health, Wealth, and Happiness*
- *Novice to Expert: 6 Steps to Learn Anything, Increase Your Knowledge, and Master New Skills*
- *Declutter Your Mind: How to Stop Worrying, Relieve Anxiety, and Eliminate Negative Thinking*
- *The Miracle Morning for Writers: How to Build a Writing Ritual That Increases Your Impact and Your Income*
- *10-Minute Declutter: The Stress-Free Habit for Simplifying Your Home*
- *The Accountability Manifesto: How Accountability Helps You Stick to Goals*
- *Confident You: An Introvert's Guide to Success in Life and Business*
- *Exercise Every Day: 32 Tactics for Building the Exercise Habit (Even If You Hate Working Out)*
- *The Daily Entrepreneur: 33 Success Habits for Small Business Owners, Freelancers and Aspiring 9-to-5 Escape Artists*
- *Master Evernote: The Unofficial Guide to Organizing Your Life with Evernote (Plus 75 Ideas for Getting Started)*

- *Bad Habits No More: 25 Steps to Break Any Bad Habit*
- *Habit Stacking: 97 Small Life Changes That Take Five Minutes or Less*
- *To-Do List Makeover: A Simple Guide to Getting the Important Things Done*
- *23 Anti-Procrastination Habits: How to Stop Being Lazy and Overcome Your Procrastination*
- *S.M.A.R.T. Goals Made Simple: 10 Steps to Master Your Personal and Career Goals*
- *Writing Habit Mastery: How to Write 2,000 Words a Day and Forever Cure Writer's Block*
- *Daily Inbox Zero: 9 Proven Steps to Eliminate Email Overload*
- *Wake Up Successful: How to Increase Your Energy and Achieve Any Goal with a Morning Routine*
- *10,000 Steps Blueprint: The Daily Walking Habit for Healthy Weight Loss and Lifelong Fitness*

Made in the USA
Lexington, KY
16 January 2019